Alexander Glass
December, 1976

NO PAT ANSWERS

D1350475

Other books by Eugenia Price

BELOVED WORLD
GOD SPEAKS TO WOMEN TODAY
MAKE LOVE YOUR AIM
SHARE MY PLEASANT STONES
THE UNIQUE WORLD OF WOMEN
WOMAN TO WOMAN
JUST AS I AM
WHERE GOD OFFERS FREEDOM

NO PAT ANSWERS

Eugenia Price

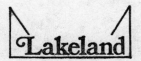

LAKELAND
BLUNDELL HOUSE
GOODWOOD ROAD
LONDON SE14 6BL

© Eugenia Price 1972

All rights reserved. No part of this
publication may be reproduced, stored
in a retrieval system, or transmitted,
in any form or by any means, electronic,
mechanical, photocopying, recording or
otherwise, without the prior permission
of the Copyright owner.

*Published in USA by Zondervan Publishing
House, Grand Rapids, Michigan.*

First British Edition 1972

ISBN 0 551 05247 3 (cased)
ISBN 0 551 00396 0 (paperback)

Made and printed in Great Britain by
Cox & Wyman Ltd., London, Reading and
Fakenham

To Eleanor and Noel Ratelle . . .
my courageous friends from whom
I have learned so much.

Contents

What To Expect

If you have always believed the "pat" theory that those who disobey God are going to suffer tragedies—disappointments, pain, hardships—and that those who obey will somehow be protected, then this book may shock you, although *No Pat Answers* is not being written to disturb, to shock, or to confuse. I am writing it because I have been forced (by the realities of my own life and life around me, and by what I have found in the Scriptures over a period of twenty-three years) to believe what is here.

And some of the things I've learned during the past few years are that evangelical Christians are not afraid to *think*, to question; are far less shockable than before; are far more interested in discovering a wider place in which to live and let live—at the same time freeing themselves to be more useful to God. Barriers are falling down all around us, and the Lord must be shouting, "Hurray!"

I know I am.

Part of my reason for exuberance is scriptural: Jesus said He came to bring a more abundant life, and life cannot be lived abundantly inside a cramped mind.

In these pages I have developed what I consider one of the biggest restrictions believers have put upon their Lord: "Pat answers" which do not jibe with the way life is. Some of us, at least, have been *restricting* God by demanding that He give us "pat answers" to the disappointments, hardships, failures, and suffering from which no one is totally exempt. Freed of any attempt to explain God or to restrict Him by refusing to ask or admit to honest questions, I remain free. Once I make even the slightest effort to force Him into a "pat answer" concerning a crisis which may have happened to me along the Way, inevitably the space around me narrows, my step slows, and my feet become entangled in the tough old vines and briar hoops of my former confusions.

I am aware that many of you have believed in and found comfort from the biblically based theory that God sends trials in order to perfect us. I do not reject this. Who am I to reject anything which gives comfort? But I, for one, can envision such devastating heartbreak in my own life that to imagine God thinking up a masochistic trial in order to test me would drive me deeper into despair. Yet, I *have* learned, have been "perfected", according to my willingness to reject self-pity, from every troubled time. My theme in these pages is simply this: What might happen if we *stopped* restricting the creativity of God by giving up the demand for receiving *or* giving "pat answers" which *we interpret as being God's own?*

Aren't we dabbling in divine *mystery* when we attempt to come up with a "spiritual" explanation for the accidental death of a high-spirited young girl, while a ninety-three-year-old man lies in a crowded nursing home almost unaware that his worn, emaciated body is being kept alive? Aren't we putting words into God's mouth when we try, either through desperation or dogmatic insistence, to "explain", even with Scripture, that God has a humanly understandable *reason* for all tragedy? All failure? All suffering?

When we attempt to unlock the mystery of the *why* of human suffering with simplistic answers or explanations, aren't we entering into spiritual superficiality as well as spiritual unreality? ". . . my ways are higher than your ways and my thoughts than your thoughts," God said. I don't believe for one minute that He said this in order to exalt Himself or to trim us down to size. He said it because it is *true*. Jesus *did* become one of us. God Himself, through His Son, got into the mess with us. No one ever need doubt the loving intentions of the Father again because Jesus ". . . hath revealed Him."

Still, there looms the unexplained *mystery* of suffering which causes us to cry out for an explanation which we can understand. Our hearts break, and we demand an answer. This is human. It is not necessarily sinful, just human. But as we make these demands upon God, aren't we also making it harder for ourselves? Wouldn't it be simpler (not easier, *simpler*) if we could, by faith, leap across this *mystery*? I have heard it said that the saints asked—not *why*, but *why not*?

Well, I'm afraid that, too, would only drive me deeper into the despair of my dark hour. If you're anything like me, what you don't need when your heart is breaking or your mind shrinking with fear is a challenge to greater "spirituality". What we need then is *hope*. Hope that, after some time has passed, by God's grace and love we can begin to live again—to function again as whole persons. A "pat answer" might temporarily placate us. At least it could set aside a few of our marginal questions. But from the beginning of time man has searched for the answer to the *why* of human tragedy—without finding it.

If God is love, I don't see Him intentionally keeping us in the dark. He must have a higher, more redemptive, more creative way of being "the God of all comfort" when we need Him. A quick answer in words we can understand might calm us for a while, but where would it take us in the final analysis? How far along the Way would it move us?

In the first throes of tragedy, we rush at God with our questions, and I firmly believe that He welcomes them. Indeed, I imagine He expects them. After all, no one but God knows us as we really are inside. Still, when we get back only what we, in our sorrow, fear, or panic, recognize as silence, what of that? Is that all we can expect from "the God of all comfort?"

It may be all we can expect by way of *understanding* the reason for our grief, shock, or fear. Could this be where we make our big mistake? Do we fall victim to *time* itself? Do we rush at God in our extremity, demanding an immediate answer in understandable words — not according to God's time schedule, but because we want our question answered now with a pat answer? Explicit—in a manner we can grasp without much concentration? Doesn't it occur to us that when tragedy strikes we are likely to be unable to think straight? Why would God expect us to be able to concentrate when we are too distressed even to sleep or eat?

There is another way in which *time* hampers our ability to trust God on short notice. We waste so much of it with non-essentials. How could we expect to be able to hear the voice of God in our distress when we have long ago forgotten, or never learned, to be quiet before

Him? When it has been so long since we've stopped the flurry of what we call "serving God" in order to wonder at the *mystery* of His love for us? I suppose it is not even odd that we, along with most of the twentieth century human race, expect "instant" understanding.

There is no time element involved in divine mystery, but there *is* silence in it. And we can't bear silence. We fear it. The radio or TV is flipped on the minute most of us enter a room. Yet we are told that the voice of God is "a still, small voice". He waits for our inner silence before He speaks on any subject. Possibly because *He wants what He says to be heard*. And when God speaks, He is never limited to mere words. Never, I'm sure, does He resort to "hard sell", repetitious, pat answers. I find, after time spent in the silence—conscious of God's eternal consciousness of me—at least a measure of understanding of why Jesus often responded to questions by asking more profound questions Himself. It isn't unusual for the "still, small voice" to respond with a question which *I* need to answer. Not that He needs my wisdom, but He knows that I need to permit perhaps one new bit of honesty to become a part of me for that day. Jesus never made speedy, simplistic replies.

The only direct statement of Jesus which is simple enough for me to comprehend when my heart is breaking or when I'm discouraged or scared is: "Follow me." I cannot understand life because life is not understandable. But I can grasp "Follow me."

In the following pages I want to tell you what those two words have come to mean to me in the troubled times which now and then clog my life and the lives of those around me. I mean to make it simple, but remember, our God is big enough for us to think about *any-thing* in His presence. His love is wide enough so that no matter how much we experiment, we will only have to follow Him in order to find ourselves led back to balance.

The next nine chapters raise the main human heart cries, the major questions we ask—the questions which we are free to ask—but to which we must, if we are to remain free in our wider place with Jesus, expect no pat answers.

And then there is the last chapter—not new—its content only too long neglected. It is called simply: *The One Answer*.

I have asked that my excess "religious litter" be cleared away as I write. Will you risk reading without yours?

EUGENIA PRICE

St. Simons Island, Georgia

Chapter 1

Disappointment

When my mother experienced a deep disappointment not long after my father died, she said: "I'm glad Daddy doesn't know about this. It would worry him to see me so upset." I disagreed with her. Had my dad still been living on this earth, he would have worried because she was disappointed. But we are told plainly in the Scriptures that once we are with God, we are like Him. I don't pretend to know what this means in its fullest sense, but I'm sure it means that *if* we are like Christ at all, we would have to be like Him in the sense of the vantage point from which He looks at everything that happens to us on earth. Great, lasting benefits, two meaningful new friendships—all sorts of creative things came out of my mother's deep disappointment. These "blessings" were (or seemed) a little long in coming, but from God's viewpoint and from the viewpoint from which my father now *sees*, time is not a factor. Creativity *is*. I don't believe for one minute that my dad was worried! He knew, seeing from his new vantage point, that eventually great good would result.

To some who read this chapter, my mother's experience in disappointment might seem to prove conclusively that the old adage: "Our disappointments are God's appointments," is true. Maybe so, but the further you read, the more you will realize my growing belief that we dare not jump to simplistic stereotyped conclusions about anything. Remember, life is *not* necessarily understandable. God must be left free to act in *His* way when disappointment strikes. Our goal here is to unlock some of our stuffy mental cupboards, too long stacked with what we may honestly believe to be "Christian answers". At least we think they are, until we try them out in the throes of a disappointment so painful that the so-called "Christian answer" spins back and hits us in the face or falls with an empty thud to the floor.

Webster defines the word *disappointment* as "the failure of expectation or hope".

We expect someone to be a certain way, to respond a certain way under a particular circumstance. Then our expectations are suddenly shattered: He or she behaves in another way entirely. A long cherished plan which, as in my mother's case, seemed so sane and practical falls through; our expectations and hopes fail, and we are helpless to do anything about it. A faithful employee has every reason to expect a raise at the end of the year and doesn't get it. A lover's hopes soar and then crash after months or even years of seeing his loved one regularly. "I had every reason on earth to believe she loved me enough to want to marry me. That she loved me as deeply as I loved her," a disappointed young man once told me. "She did enjoy being with me, but not enough to want to spend the rest of her life with me." I can still remember the stricken look on his face. A look of near disbelief, so deep was his disappointment.

Disappointment in matters of the heart is no more crushing than disappointment where one's work is concerned, *if* the work has been fulfilling and productive. With retirement only six years away, an old friend of mine was quite suddenly—and without warning—fired. Oh, he was told he could "resign", but that was the last thing he wanted, and he could not have lived with his conscience had he agreed to pretend that he was willing to leave his job. For more than twenty-five years he had given his best efforts to a large organization. Then a new man came into the firm with designs on my friend's position, and with only forty-eight hours' notice, my friend was *out*. His spirit, his inner life with Christ, was strong enough to withstand the blow without losing his mental equilibrium, but the scars still remain.

In an instance such as this, the word *disappointment* is really an understatement. There is, even with a Christian of this man's calibre, no way to escape a kind of inner shattering when one is suddenly cut off from the work which has not only been fulfilling, but which through long years of involvement has become a large part of one's identity. Intellectually, my friend knew that he was still just as good as ever in his chosen field—better than most. He knew that what had happened to him had nothing to do with his own competence; it merely had to do with someone else wanting his job—someone who resorted to trickery to gain what he wanted. Yet I watched this man bleed from the self-doubt which tore at him for months afterwards.

His mind told him he had done nothing wrong or even inferior, but his heart—his emotions—did not understand. Hard, swift disappointment breeds the feeling of rejection in all of us, and I don't think we should fight this. We dare not permit our shredded emotions, our feelings of rejection to take over, but surely during those painful first weeks, we shouldn't have to sit still while some superficial, though well-meaning person tries to convince us that we're wrong to feel rejected. Most of us know we're *wrong* to feel rejected, but as with my friend, most of us also know that the feeling of rejection is there because we've associated our inner beings with the work which has just been snatched away.

Facing this is merely common sense.

A mother, whom I don't know personally, wrote concerning her heartbreak over her son in whom she had such high hopes. Unfortunately for the boy (and for her) he had been the centre of his mother's life since the death of his father in the early days of United States' involvement in the Vietnamese War. To permit one's interests to focus completely on another person is not only unfair to that person, but to oneself. Still, it happens. And under the circumstances of this woman's life, it was as natural for her to feel rejected when her son got into trouble as it was for the man who was suddenly fired. To say this mother was unwise for having allowed her entire life to revolve around her son doesn't help. The boy had been the centre of her life for far too long to hope for a sudden change. We all do wrong, unwise things, but we're well on our way to release from disappointment or any other troubling problem when we stop pummelling ourselves and simply face facts.

The Vietnamese War widow *knew* she had been too possessive of the boy, who had now turned to drugs and had been arrested and jailed for breaking and entering in order to get more drugs. "I know our servicemen are exposed to this terrible thing called the drug habit, but my son was still in college. If only the Lord would tell me where I failed," she wrote. "If only I'd get some kind of *answer* when I pray! If only I knew *why* this dreadful thing came into my wonderful son's life! Into mine."

My heart ached, of course, as I read page after page of her letter—page after page of bitter disappointment and demand for an *answer* as to why this had to happen.

Another woman wanted to know why God would spare the life of her sister's son in Vietnam and allow *her* boy to be killed. "I prayed for my son's safety almost every hour he was over there. My sister isn't even a Christian! She doesn't believe in prayer, and yet my son is dead, and hers is back home, safe and alive. My husband and I had such dreams for our son because he was brilliant in his studies and never in any kind of trouble. Now, our dreams are buried with him."

I had no answer for either woman's question. I shared the irony in both letters. I tried desperately to identify with both mothers, but I had no answer, simply because there is none—really.

In my mail today, as I write this chapter, came a letter from one of the many persons whom I have come to know by correspondence through the years. I have never seen this young woman, but I've read letter after letter, and I do not believe her to be a chronic complainer. She happens to feel comfortable enough with me to say what she thinks, to ask all her questions *without* expecting me or anyone else to give her a pat answer. In today's letter she wrote:

"My father (a stroke victim) had a bad day yesterday. Those days are hard on us all. The doctor keeps repeating that there's nothing he can do. Dad will have to go to a nursing home eventually. This has been going on for nine years now. My dad is a vicious man anyway, and this doesn't make it any easier remembering how mean he was before the stroke ever happened. Last week my friend's father died after a short illness. He was a kind man. Everyone loved and needed him. Losing him was a real disappointment and grief to me. Sometimes things are hard to understand, aren't they?"

Yes.

This girl is not demanding an answer from me, not even a letter in reply. Writing out her questions simply helps her think things through. At any rate, in each letter I see her moving farther out into the wider place with Jesus Christ. Equally important, she is *thinking*—daring to ask her questions *in His presence*—without fear.

Disappointment does not always follow a build up of hopes or expectations. Sometimes our hopes, dreams, and expectations seem to have nothing to do with it. We may be jogging along through our days, doing our work, minding our own business when suddenly the sky falls in upon us. But it might be helpful to mention the kind of disappointment which we incur by refusing to accept a quick change in plans we've previously made—the kind of disappointment we bring on ourselves simply by acting like spoiled brats.

"I was *living* for the vacation cruise my husband promised me this year! It had been so long since we'd just gone away together in a carefree manner—for fun—instead of to a medical convention. I'd done my shopping; he'd even done his. Our luggage was partially packed, and in he comes from the hospital last night telling me we can't go! The doctor who shares his practice had a heart attack. My husband wouldn't dare leave their sick patients—but I'm so mad, I could spit!"

I heard that tale of woe in a supermarket when I still lived in Chicago. The pouting, disappointed lady as a neighbour. Her disappointment was not only vocal, it was inevitable. It was also understandable. Every husband and wife should have a chance to go away now and then—"just for fun". I felt sorry for her, but sorrier for her husband, because I was sure he wouldn't hear the last of her fuming until somehow he managed to take her on that cruise. Too much time has passed now for me to recall if the lady actually asked *why* such a letdown should come to her, but the tone of her voice implied the question.

Isn't it true that most of us don't know what to do with disappointments, either large or small? And isn't the reason because we haven't grown up enough to know? Are we still children in this area? Do some of us cling even to childhood disappointments, almost enjoying the still-lingering, bittersweet pain? We all have childhood disappointments tucked back in the usually guarded corners of our memories, and some of them *are* still painful, even after all those years—perhaps too painful to discuss. We can feel the shame or the hurt or the blow as though it had happened only yesterday. Depending upon the nature of the crisis, it is probably good to talk about it, as long as we don't *relive* it, nurturing the bitterness it left in our minds, stirring up the old silt long settled to the bottom of our memories.

"I can still hate my sister," a friend told me once, "because she laughed at me when I cried the day I opened my birthday present and found—not a doll I'd dreamed of owning, with golden curls—but a pair of shoes to wear to school! I know it's silly. My sister and I are grandmothers now, but do you know, *I can still hate her* when I let myself remember how she laughed?"

My friend and fellow writer Joyce Blackburn remembers the choking pain of two disappointing "presents" she received during her childhood years. She remembers the shattering moments, but is able to laugh as she might about a fictionalized child's experience in one of her juvenile books.

Several days before Joyce's fourth birthday, a large, mysterious box arrived from her grandmother. The box, addressed to Joyce, was pushed far back under her parents' bed for safekeeping. Joyce, of course, found it, and daily she crawled under the bed to sniff the big, exciting box. It smelled of vanilla for some strange reason, and to her child mind the best of all possible birthday gifts awaited her: A huge box of vanilla ice cream! The big doll she found when the box was finally opened made her cry. Like me, as a child she didn't care much for dolls anyway, but this one didn't stand a chance. It wasn't made of vanilla ice cream!

Not long after that disappointment, she attended a Christmas party where the children were to receive gifts. Joyce's heart had been set on a "witch watch". The minute she walked into the room where the big tree stood, her eye fell on a toy wrist watch tied to a branch within her reach. When the time came for each child to select a toy from the tree, she quickly took the watch and as quickly felt it grabbed from her hands by a freckled-faced little boy. Her disappointment turned to instant grief. I don't doubt at all that a child could know real grief at a moment like that. "I can still feel it," she declares. "I thought my heart would break." The worst blow of all came, though, when some thoughtless adult—instead of making the boy return her watch—took the easy way (for the adult) and gave the boy's present to Joyce. "It was a horrid little yellow taxi-cab."

The healthy adult can chuckle over childhood stories such as these, but there is nothing funny at the time about the disappointment of a child, or of an adult, especially when there is a reminder around to keep the lost hope or the smashed dream alive.

In *Lighthouse*, chronologically the first in my St. Simons Island trilogy of novels, James Gould, disappointed in love when a Scottish lass married his brother, fled from New England to St. Simons Island, Georgia. Was he a coward? Should he have stayed in the North in the same Massachusetts town where the sight of his brother and the girl would keep his disappointment alive? Or did he do the sensible thing by running away in search of a new life for himself? Who knows? Many of us have no choice anyway. Few can get away from the scene of the smashed dream, the lost hope, as James Gould did. And certainly none of us can escape disappointment.

Why do some lives seem marked with more than their normal share? I don't know. There *is* no answer to that question. Is a tragedy-scarred life, such as the life of Rose Kennedy, really an indication that God knows of a special inner strength in her? That He can trust her to be stronger than most women? I don't know. I've heard that pat answer over and over again, as you have, I'm sure. Not only about Rose Kennedy, but about other courageous, crisis-filled lives. Such a concept must be of some vague comfort to the person whose days seem to see no end of grief and trouble, but I also know of both men and women who are now in mental institutions because their spirits and their minds broke in the face of repeated disappointment. Does God love them any less?

Aren't we simply on the wrong track to demand an answer? An explanation? Even a theory?

What about our attempts to shield those we love from disappointment? We can do this now and then, you know. I learned of a wife who handled the entire ghastly business of an Internal Revenue Service tax examination while her husband was away. In making out their joint return, the man had made an enormous error, and she knew his self-confidence would crack if he found out about it before the matter was settled. She paid the additional tax due, and her husband didn't discover his mistake until he began to work over their returns the next year. The woman had set her heart on buying new living-room furniture with that additional tax money, but her own disappointment was easier to bear than to watch his.

There are times, of course, when we can harm those we love by over-protecting, by attempting to spare them momentary disappointment. Dreading to hurt, we lie or gloss over, but in the long run the pain and disappointment may only run deeper.

My fiction editor, Miss Tay Hohoff, without whom I would still hesitate to tackle an historical novel, could have spared me a temporary disappointment during the writing of *Lighthouse*. We had decided, tentatively, upon a place to begin the story. I did my research and began. In fact, although I didn't feel it was rolling easily, I "roughed in" over three hundred pages before

I sent a sample to Tay for her opinion. Writing is seldom easy, and so I kept telling myself, "Either you're a pro or you're not a pro. Keep going. Tay is very busy right now. Just keep going." After months of hard work, before leaving for a two-weeks' trip with Mother and her neighbours, I retyped about a hundred pages and sent them to her. My trip was nearly perfect. I was rested and refreshed by it—and a good thing I was! When I reached my home on St. Simons Island, there was the big brown envelope with my hundred pages and a long, loving, but straight-from-the-shoulder letter from Tay: "Genie, dear . . . This is a difficult letter to write, but it has to be done. There is *very little* about these first pages that I really can applaud." And then she began to explain where I had failed. There was no hope of simply *rewriting*. The place I had chosen to begin was wrong. Nothing could save the manuscript but an entirely new start! I felt as though I had been kicked in the head. Mother and her two friends were to be my house guests for almost a week, so I took one of them, my close friend Nancy Goshorn, into my confidence, but I did not tell Mother. She knew I was behind schedule anyway. Why ruin her vacation?

What I did do was flee to my desk alone and lay it on the line with Jesus Christ: "You know, Lord, that *I can't do this and still make my deadline*. I'm not experienced enough as a novelist. I just can't do it. So, You'll have to take over. I'm dumping the whole thing in Your lap, and I also have to trust You to free me enough from this disappointment so Mother won't make use of that ESP of hers and catch on. I can't start to work again for a week. So, here it is."

I did make that deadline, and once I found the right

place to start, the manuscript came to life. What if Tay Hohoff had not been so wise? "I can't be any good to you," she wrote at the end of her long letter of criticism, "if I'm not honest with you." I shuddered the day I read her letter, but I shudder more now when I think what might have happened had she been weak enough to have tried to protect me from that initial disappointment.

That happened to be the type of disappointment which can bring panic. The panic I felt until I got alone with God was nothing compared to what I might have experienced had I known (as He did) that in a little more than two months my friend and housemate, Joyce Blackburn, was going to have emergency surgery, *and* right at deadline time in February, Mother was going to slip on her kitchen floor and break her leg! Is there a clue for us here? Not only where disappointments are concerned, but as a substitute for a pat answer, might it not help if we remember that God knows what has happened *and* what is going to happen? That He does have His own way of working in our disappointments and heartaches—*not* discounting the element of *time*, but rather by making use of it? He gave me such peace the day the letter came that I was able to pick up the telephone and tell Tay not to worry—I was fine! Did that unexpected, almost unbelievable gift of peace give me the added energy I needed to complete the job in spite of the trouble still ahead for me? Did the stretching of my own heart during the final stages make the book better? I don't know. I can vouch for this much: not once during either Joyce's or Mother's suffering did the question *why?* arise in my heart. God never gives false peace, and I'm just as impatient and capable of jitters as you are; sometimes, I think, too conscientious about deadlines. Why *did* these two persons who mean so much to me have to fall ill right when I could so little afford the time away from the book? Again, I don't know. I don't need to know. I only know that as I started all over, I had *hope* of making it. I had been *given* hope along with peace.

Christians know, or are supposed to know, that there *is* hope in God. I don't think of hope as coming *from* God, but as *in God*. He is not a zillion light years away, reaching "down" to hand us a little package of *hope*. He is here, and hope is *in Him*. Nowhere in the New Testament did Jesus ever hint that His followers would be protected from disappointment. Placing one's faith in Jesus Christ in no way guarantees an insurance policy against smashed dreams or blighted expectations. Disappointment is a real part of every life. I don't believe for one minute that God intended it to be that way when He created man, but there is the matter of the Fall. Man did act on his own in spite of God's warning, and ever since then there has been disappointment to live through, to work around, to try to understand or forget.

None of our disappointments escape God's notice, but in the New Testament I find nothing which indicates that He will do us the injustice of a fatherly explanation as to *why* this special disappointment came our way. "In this world, ye shall have tribulations. . . ."

Those are Jesus' own words. God in Jesus Christ has shown Himself to be a complete realist. There simply is no pat answer to disappointment, so isn't it time we began to free God by calling a halt to our demands for one? The Lord is not obtuse. He does *not try* to be

27

difficult. The problem may lie with us, with our earth-bound inability to see trouble from the viewpoint of eternity as God sees it. But if I could see all things from His vantage point, would I need Him?

Could it be that we, especially during our trials, simply need to believe that God always acts in the way of love towards us?

Do we judge God's love by the disappointments in our lives instead of by what we know of Jesus Christ—who *is* a Redeemer God? And who is *never late* with *being* the real answer to our needs?

Chapter 2

Disillusionment

How different is the experience of *disillusionment* from the experience of *disappointment*? Isn't disillusionment the loss of faith in something or someone? Doesn't disillusionment usually follow disappointment? Yes. But it implies a great deal more involvement on our part. Spoiled, immature adults are often disappointed simply because they expect too many good things to come to them. Still, many of life's merely *disappointing* experiences are not our fault. The line here is so fine as to be almost invisible, but perhaps it's safe to say that when we are *disillusioned*, often the fault *does* lie with us. However, disillusionment is painful, no matter who causes our illusions to crumble. Illusions, at best, are—illusions. Natural to the young, but dangerous for most of us.

The word *illusion* is defined as "the state of being intellectually deceived, deluded, or misled". Doesn't sound desirable, does it? And yet how many times have you heard people click their tongues and despair that someone has lost his or her illusions? Faith in humanity? I see no way for the young to avoid illusions, but they are shaky ground for anyone, and deadly in adults. Shaky, deadly, yet unavoidable for us all, if we are honest. Unavoidable and unreal. And disillusionment in the young or old can lead to some of our most painful moments. To say one ought not to be intellectually deceived or fooled, to say one ought not to put his trust in man or in man-made insitutions, to say one ought only to put trust in God, helps very little when the first shock of disillusionment strikes.

Some disillusioning experiences come gradually, but more often than not the element of shock is involved when an idol crumbles, a dream disintegrates, a hope vanishes.

A woman in her thirties, obviously writing in a state of shock, told me about her middle-aged minister whom she had revered. "He made God so real to me; I found myself anxious for Sunday to come so I could hear Rev. . . . . . . preach about Him again. My minister was not only a man with the look of heaven on his face; he treated us all as though he had heaven in his heart too. I found Christ under his teaching, and I thought he could do no wrong. I knew he had to be the kind of Christian he convinced me I could be if I fully surrendered my life to God. Why, I even stopped smoking because my minister suggested it. My husband and I both thought the sun rose and set in this man of God. And then . . ."

The letter continued with the tragic story of the minister's fall from his pedestal. I was sorry for my correspondent, but my heart bled for the minister! He had been dismissed from his church because he was caught in the act of seducing the church organist. Now, this has happened before, and it will happen again. Ministers *are* men of God, but they are mere men too, and I pitied him more than I pitied my correspondent because he had a triple hurdle to leap over: The loss of work he undoubtedly loved, the unavoidable humiliation and shame, *and* the recovery by Grace of his self-respect for the future.

The lady who wrote to me? She had one hurdle, but that one could be hard to clear. In the first place, most of us don't want to clear it. We prefer to put our faith in people whom we can see, hear, and adore—in person. Watching an idol crack up and fall into dust and pieces around our feet is a marvellous excuse for a luxurious dive into self-pity. "I went right back to smoking," the woman wrote.

Well, she didn't hurt the poor, already troubled minister. I'm sure he was so blinded by the fury of his own problems that he lost no sleep at all because she went back to a habit she had stopped—apparently only for him. She was wounding and rewounding herself because it seemed to her that somehow she had a *right* to her illusions about her minister. Was he to blame? Yes. Certainly he had not made God clear to her. He had made himself clear. At least, he had not stopped her from forming a false image. Obviously, he had not shown her that if any man on earth had been perfect or without sin, Jesus would not have needed to die. She had not been taught that it is not only unrealistic, but also dangerously unthinking for anyone to put his faith so utterly in any human being, no matter how good he may appear—no matter how good he really is. No man is good enough, no woman is good enough for that kind of confidence. In fact, we do them harm in the long run by expecting them not to be human. My mixed-up correspondent felt deeply sorry for herself. Her pain was real; she was truly *dis*illusioned. But I wrote back: "Hurray! Now you can begin to see clearly. Now you never need be mixed up about God again. Now you can begin to 'love your neighbour as yourself,' providing this unhappy experience also causes you to begin to be realistic about *you* too. You and the minister are fellow sinners, with access to the same forgiveness."

Disillusionment leaves a bitter taste in the heart and the mind. It causes intense pain, and sometimes shame that we were so foolish, but I'm not about to criticize those who crash from their pedestals. I'll leave that for someone with more authority than I in dealing with the overt sins of the human heart. What I want to clarify is that unlike *disappointment, disillusionment can* always work for our good, for our freedom, for our spiritual maturity.

Before I go further, let it be known that I agree with St. Paul who warned us against causing our weaker brothers and sisters to stumble. I have not defended this wayward minister, but I have prayed for him. I see the kind of man he can still be by Grace. Neither do I condemn the poor woman whose illusions he shattered. I pity her, but the moment of disillusionment for her can, if she will agree, become a wide-swung door into freedom from attempting to live the Christian life without having her eyes on Jesus Christ Himself. I pray that she picked up my "Hurray!" and ran with it through that open door.

There are as many forms of *disillusionment* as there are people capable of being disillusioned. Some are deadly serious; others are not. Some are dangerous; others are less so. And some are downright ridiculous.

Joyce Blackburn and I don't live by a strict division of household chores. If I am working against a manuscript deadline, she does the errands. If she is hard-pressed for time, I do them. Not long ago, wearing a pair of old blue jeans, I was shopping for our groceries when, going too fast, as always, with my loaded market cart, I nearly collided with a lady and her cart at the scouring powder shelf. We both said "excuse me", and I went on hunting my favourite brand. In a moment, I realized the lady was still standing by her cart, staring at me. "Could you be Eugenia Price?" I admitted I was, and there followed the (for me) awkward moment when she gasped: "I—I've read all your novels about this beautiful island and—well, seeing you here buying scouring powder—well, I just can't believe it!"

Like the minister, I disillusion a lot of people merely by being human, I suppose. To a certain kind of romantic reader, authors evidently are supposed to wear flowing garments instead of blue jeans and find other means of keeping their sinks clean without scouring powder.

Every so often I receive a letter of "disillusionment" from some reader who has blithely driven past my Private Road sign all the way to my locked gate. "What kind of Christian are you to lock yourself away from the public like that?" Of course, they almost always tell me how much they've been helped by one book or another, and there I sit wondering how they think I'd ever get those books written if I kept myself available to the dozen or more carloads of people who appear daily at my big old farm gate?

When Joyce Blackburn appeared at a Children's Book Fair some time ago, appearing also was Henry Aaron, the great home run hitter of the Atlanta Braves. Joyce was delighted to meet and talk with Mr. Aaron in person, but what stuck in her memory was the look of sheer adoration on the faces of the children when they shook his hand and then whispered: "Hank, could I see your callouses?" There they were—splendid, thick callouses from swinging that famous record-breaking bat. And there were the open, trusting faces of those children. What a responsibility Hank Aaron carries! With one unkind word, he could scar a boy's character. With one evening's ungentlemanly conduct in public, he could influence a youngster. Exaggerated? I don't think so, if the child who holds his precious illusions about Mr. Aaron is young enough—impressionable enough. Henry Aaron is a man of "exemplary conduct", but being a thoughtful gentleman, he must find the burden heavy at times.

The illusions of children are not silly; they are natural. But it is another matter when we reach the twenties, thirties, forties, and, like me, the fifties, still clinging to unrealistic illusions, still insisting upon putting our faith in people.

I will never, never forget the stricken look on the pale, drawn face of a man who stopped me one night after a speaking engagement some years ago. At first, he asked for nothing except that I pray for him. I said I would, and then he said, as though he surprised himself in the telling: "You see, my wife shot herself when she found out I'd had an affair with another woman. The affair was over seven years before. But I—I guess when my wife found out—just last winter—it was too much for her." He fell silent. With enormous effort, he tried to smile and failed. "The—the note she left only said that she couldn't live being so disillusioned with me." Tears were running down his cheeks. "I guess—she—worshipped me."

I had to agree with him. What else could one say to a man expected to carry that burden for the remainder of his earthly life? Only that he could rest his heart about her now because at last she knew who it was she should have been worshipping all along.

You see, the word *worship* only fits one place and one *person*. The word itself implies that the object of that worship be deserving. More than that, it implies that the object of our worship *draws* complete, yielded, totally reverent adoration from us. As the years go by, I am more and more convinced that St. Paul was right when he wrote of the day when ". . . at the Name of Jesus, every knee will bow". Every knee will bow because no one who sees Him as He is can *not* worship! In that sense, the choice is almost taken from us. And yet choice is there. Mainly, I suppose, because no one can get to know God in Jesus Christ well enough for this inevitable kind of worship without first surrendering to Him.

Once I worked at whipping up a feeling I could call "worship". No more, I have lived consciously in His presence long enough to know Him, to recognize His pressure on my heart and mind. We've been together long enough so that fixing supper, changing the ribbon in my typewriter, and riding a bike around my shell road have become almost sacramental. This does not indicate my "holiness". It indicates His—His holiness and His drawing power for my heart or for yours.

"I, if I be lifted up . . . will draw all men unto me," Jesus said. We are drawn to other people, to a sunset, to a clear, black shadow across grass, to a passage of music, but only God can draw us to real *worship*. Any other form of worship is false and will end in disillusionment.

Only Jesus Christ *cannot* disillusion us. It is not that He *will* not, but that He *cannot*.

"I'm so disillusioned with the organized church." Good! There is nothing in the Scriptures which tells us we are to have any illusions whatever about the church made up of much-organized human beings. Shattered illusions about anything man-made can give us reason to shout "Hurray!" Reality cannot be built on unreality.

One day my kind and gentlemanly neighbour, Mr. Curtis Stevens, began bulldozing through his woods which adjoin my property. When I discovered that he wasn't going to build anything, I was horrified that such a gentle, lovely man, who enjoyed the wild stands of woods as much as I, would tear into them in such a violent manner. Being Curtis Stevens he smiled and explained quietly that he had always been taught to keep his woods clean. 'You see, Eugenia," he said, "those big trees you love so much have to have some of the scrub trees and undergrowth cleared away periodically so the real trees cannot only be seen, but be fed." I listened, still perplexed, staring down into the tangled mess of mud, uprooted gums, pines, and myrtles. Finally, I managed, "But don't you think the light is beautiful, Curtis, when it cuts down through those dear little scrub oaks and myrtles?" He smiled. "Yes, I do. But you wait until I'm through, and then you'll see something really beautiful—as soon as these scars are gone. Right now we only have the *illusion* of woods."

Immediately after his clean-up job, my heart sank every time I rounded a certain curve in the little sandy road I had cut over an easement through Mr. Stevens' property. That curve, I thought, was ruined by those gaping open spaces. But do you know something? Curtis

Stevens was right. Land "goes back to woods" fast where I live, and already—within only a few months—I look forward to rounding that one curve I thought had been desecrated forever! My wise neighbour got rid of the "illusion of woods", left the big oaks and pines and hickories, and now they stand in pools of light. Now we have real woods and more light.

Disillusionment is painful, but ultimately it can be good. George Santayana said, "Wisdom comes by disillusionment." And true wisdom is in Jesus Christ. Only He *cannot* disillusion us.

Chapter 3

Failure

Consider this list of words: Unsuccess, non-success, unfulfilment, non-fulfilment, forlorn hope, miscarriage, misfire, abortion, fizzle (*colloq.*), flop (*slang*), collapse, debacle, fiasco, dud (colloq.), washout (colloq.), bankruptcy, insolvency, crash, smash, wreck, ruin, fall, downfall.

This is the *New Roget's Thesaurus* list of synonyms for what we think of as *failure*, and it's pretty complete. In fact, it seems to grow more terrifying as it goes along. "Flop . . . fiasco . . . smash . . . ruin."

One of America's great moral weaknesses could be her refusal to accept anything resembling *failure*. Men who do not succeed simply have no place in our society. I suppose the indictment should not be limited to America, for the entire Western Civilization is success happy. But in America success carries a big whip—a long, stinging whip which begins to strike even small children who are coerced into contests of all kinds and are punished, pushed, pushed to win. Not to fail—to win.

Of course, no one should ever be urged to fail. That is ridiculous. One should only be urged to do one's best—succeed or fail in the process. On paper all of this seems so obvious; I wonder at my need to set it down. And yet I, along with you and most of the people we know, have spent my life trying not to fail. The first humiliating failure I remember occurred when I was about ten years old. I flunked mathematics, and I wanted to die, because my grades in school were my pride and joy. I remember crying into my pillow at night with the bitter sting of guilt I carried from that failure.

My second humiliating failure had to do with what the educational system used to call the Palmer Method. This, as some of you will recall, was the devil's own device for torturing children who just didn't happen to be born with fingers adept at making "round and round" circles and "push-pull" marks time after time and page after page with nary a line misplaced. The idea was to "rubber rubber" when you wrote, somehow rolling your forearm on the inner muscle and holding the pen just so as you rolled. The most frightening part of it was the Palmer Method Lady, a veritable frigate of a woman, who came to my classroom and sailed haughtily up and down between the rows of desks, peering approvingly or disdainfully down at what we victims were attempting. She scared the living daylights out of me! Even worse than her rubber heels which kept me from guessing where she would appear next was the smile she gave to the students who could perform that weird ritual with pen, ink, and paper and the snorts we failures received.

I don't think it mattered one bit whether or not I could make all those circles and push-pulls without a line misplaced or without spilling a blob of ink every time I managed to reach almost the last page. Still, I was made to believe that if I *failed*, something was dreadfully wrong with me.

None of this is intended as a diatribe against education. I only mention these incidents here because the suffering I experienced at my *failures* is relevant.

It was genuine suffering. I doubt that it marked me, since my young mother happened to be enlightened beyond her time and kept reminding me that making those "round and rounds" and "push-pulls" need not affect the success of my future life. She had wisdom enough to teach my brother and me that we might not succeed in everything we tackled, but we could always do our best.

Lewis E. Lawes once wrote: "Never give a man up until he has failed at something he likes." Do you agree with that? I don't. I see his intent, but I don't agree. In fact, I think we fail at doing many things we *like*. I like to write books, but they are not all huge successes. I like to make new friends and have time and a rested mind to answer my mail with care, but I often fail to budget my time in order to accomplish these things *which I like*. I try, and sometimes I succeed, but more often than not I fail to find time and a back rested enough from having worked on a manuscript or answered "duty" mail. I fail myself and I fail my friends.

So do you, I'm sure.

We all fail our families, our neighbours, and our friends when we refuse to take care of our health. I am failing my mother and everyone else who loves me when I repeatedly allow myself to gain a dozen extra pounds of fat! Right now, I've got it pretty well licked (with my physician's approval), thanks to Dr. Stillman's *Quick Weight Loss Diet*, but no one knows better than I that I can fizzle again. We are all adept at being fiascos, wash-outs, duds, flops.

I was interested in finding the words *insolvency* and *bankruptcy* in the *Thesaurus* list of synonyms for *failure*. The mother of a friend of mine, left with insurmountable debts after the death of her husband, had to declare bankruptcy. The daughter described the particular shame and agony of such a procedure so graphically that I suffered along with them. "Forlorn hope" surrounds such an experience, I'm sure. We have read and heard about—perhaps known—men who took their own lives rather than declare bankruptcy. The suffering from this kind of failure could easily drive a proud man to his death—or a proud woman for that matter. In us all is at least the potential for drastic action when we face the panic of no funds.

Last year a woman wrote asking why God didn't spare her husband who had, according to her letter, "died of a broken heart" because he had failed at his business and could no longer face seeing his wife and children suffer because of his failure. She wanted me to give her a definite answer, and, of course, I couldn't. Her letter was just another affirmation of what I am attempting to communicate in this book.

As I see it, God had nothing directly to do with her husband's death or his failure. God set into motion certain genetic laws, and some among us inherit "smart business sense" while others do not. Fortune, good and bad, is also a factor. Bad breaks come into the lives of Christians as well as non-Christians. One of the gentlest, kindest, most loving Christian men I know just can't seem to make it in his chosen field. In fact, he's tried all sorts of other fields and failed in those too.

Why? Is there a pat answer here? Is his faith too small? In this man's case, *no*. But what of the glib prosperous Christian businessmen who *insist* upon "giving God the glory"? I purposely italicized that word "insist", because these fellows talk and write so much about how 'God is blessing them" that they make me suspicious! Their pious talk has the ring of relieving *them* of some of the blame for all those amassed fortunes. It's almost as though they're saying, "Well, I can't help being so rich and getting richer. I tithe, and the good Lord does the rest."

Now, I ask you—why would God deliberately prosper one tithing Christian over another? Would God cause one devout brother to fail at everything he tries *only* in order to strengthen that brother's faith? Doesn't God care about strengthening the faith of the prospering brother too? Does God play favourites? Would the Lord God "bless" one business with so much profit that the children of the boss can zoom around our highways in sports cars while the children of another equally spiritual man lack money for school supplies?

The idea is ridiculous.

But we are more ridiculous when we attempt to confine God's activity in any life *to our understanding* of what may be happening. The New Testament is there for us to read—to read and re-read—but I dare you to find one line in it which implies that God is going to grant special favours for faith in Himself. In the Old Testament, yes; but its great value is that it moves relentlessly towards the New. Jesus came to reveal God as He is, not as we wish Him to be. Jesus came to make God plain: to clarify the universal human need for a Saviour and to *be* that Saviour. But in His coming, He also said: "In this world ye shall have tribulation. . . ." Not once did He even intimate that He and the Father had special favourites among us. Jesus came to earth as a helpless baby, born into the family of a man and woman of moderate means. He lived penniless, slept on hillsides and in borrowed beds, and ate what people gave Him to eat.

Why, if material "blessings" and financial prosperity are God's way of showing His love, would His only begotten Son, Jesus Christ, have had to be buried in a borrowed tomb?

I went "round the bush" on this subject with a wealthy man who is also a sincere Christian. He gave me the old bromide about gratitude. "Genie, aren't we to give God the glory? Aren't we to give thanks?"

Of course, we are to give God the glory. Of course, we are to give thanks. But St. Paul did say, "In *everything* give thanks. . . ." I've never yet heard a man thank God for a business failure or the loss of an investment, have you? It has been said that "Sometimes a noble failure serves the world as faithfully as a distinguished success." I believe that, but few of us speak of our "noble failures". Mainly, I think, because we have been taught *not* to fail, and if we do, to keep it a secret. We have been led to believe that there is shame in failure. What about Jesus? Wasn't He considered a failure by the world in which He lived? His promised kingdom did not materialize at all—at least not in the way the people expected it. And isn't this the key to the problem of failure?

Does God measure blessings in dollars and cents, or does He measure them in kingdom terms? Jesus brought the potential for an inward kingdom, a rule for the peoples of the earth so predicated on love that the *inner being* of every man who embraced it could be untangled—freed to reach towards his fellows.

Great riches complicate. I'm far from rich now, but sometimes I almost long for the old days when I had no taxes to pay, no interest rates to worry about, and no accountant to keep me in Uncle Sam's good graces. Making even a fair living complicates so many things that I will never believe God equates this kind of so-called success with a "blessing". He came to simplify, not to complicate.

Another area in which women, in particular, struggle with failure is the matter of childlessness. Well, this has tormented a certain type of woman since the days of Abraham's Sarah. But here again we need to be realistic, to stop leaning on old clichés. Does God send every child who is born into the world? Our world is in desperate danger of disaster because we *do* have a population explosion on our hands Not only are millions of children going hungry, but cities the world over are frantically hunting ways to dispose of the waste created by the people we already have. Does God care about the environment He created for earth people? Does He care about the hungry children? Doesn't God know about the conditions now existing from over-population? Is He really "blessing" the poor family with twelve children and "depriving" another well-to-do man and wife of even one child? Don't you honestly think God is more balanced it His viewpoint? Wouldn't He find it more creative if some of the affluent childless couples adopted and fed and clothed a few of the underprivileged children who will otherwise never know normal, healthy lives?

Isn't it foolish to nurse a sense of failure at being childless when God's kind of creativity could remedy it?

Now, I'm sure someone is going to be furious or hurt because I have said God does not "send" children into the world. I did not say that, of course. But I do hope we will free God from always having to act according to what we've believed or taken for granted about Him. Children interest me very much. I see what Jesus meant when He urged us to be like them. And I'm sure when two people love each other in Christ that His hand is in the wonder of the coming of their children. Still, do we dare go on being so pat about Him? Would these childless women feel they were such failures if they looked around at the over-populated world and the starving children in it?

There is really only one point to be made here. We can neither blame nor praise God for our blessings *or* failures until we have opened our minds enough to let *His* sanity take over. Is sanity too strong a word? I don't think so, but how about clear-sightedness? God sees clearly into each human heart and mind and into each circumstance.

The God who flung the heavens into space, the planets into orbit—the God who created violets and waving Spanish moss won't be confined to any human concept. It is, of course, our distorted concept of Him which goes into that pat answer we concoct, and it is we who are the losers when we do not find Him exactly as *we* decided He should be.

Everyone fails at something, or he has made no effort. Only those who make no effort are exempt. Failure is an integral part of being alive. Success can be, too, but

Jesus didn't come to this earth to scatter blessings and success among the faithful. He came so that everyone could find out what the Father is really like.

Chapter 4

Grief

Aubrey Thomas DeVere, the Irish poet, once wrote: "Grief should be like joy: majestic, sedate, confirming, cleansing, equable, making free, strong to consume small troubles, to command great thoughts, thoughts lasting to the end."

Do you believe that? I can accept the ultimate meaning, but are thoughts such as the poet's even possible when the grief through which we struggle to survive is so great that it is unspeakable? Inexpressible? Even by tears?

Shakespeare believed that "Everyone can master a grief but he that has it." I find that easier to swallow, but I simply don't see that grief is to be mastered. It is to be lived through as creatively as possible, but not mastered. However, we dare not permit grief to master us. Doesn't it make far more sense if we attempt to find out how grief can be *used* rather than *wasted*? How we can be creative *in it*, not destroyed by it?

Many years ago I slowly, almost hesitantly, began to grasp the truth of what was then to me a revolutionary concept in E. Stanley Jones' great book, *Christ and Human Suffering*: that because, in Jesus, God is showing Himself to be a Redeemer, then why cannot He also redeem human suffering by giving us a way to make use of it?

"Develop the concept, Genie," Stanley Jones said. "It comes from the Father in the first place, and He always gives freely. Not to me more than to you. Our part is only to be there to receive."

Anyone who has read one or more of my books in the past decade has found this concept running like a bright thread through those explorations—explorations which for me have been unavoidable. It has been as though I were pushed to discover and then communicate—at least in part—my fragmentary insights into what actually may be God's way of involvement in human suffering. Not only the extent of His involvement (which I now believe to be entire), but how we are to lay hold of His help in time of trouble. More than once I have tried to back away from the exploration. When any grief is fresh, even the most well-intentioned attempt to lessen it can irritate, disturb, and confuse. Yet I have not been able to move in any direction except *towards* a gradually growing certainty that not only is God involved in our griefs, but He also has a *use* for them. He waits until we are able to think and then begins His action *through* our sorrows.

The lengths of God's waiting time vary according to the personality of the one who has come to Him for help. The variant is not on God's side; it is on ours. He is always ready to begin the redemptive process. After all, He *is* a Redeemer God. The variants are ours because we are all different in the swiftness or slowness with which we grasp truth and are able to act on it.

After months of conscientiously trying to live through her grief following her mother's death, Frances, one of my dear friends, wrote: "For over two months now, I have been mostly what I call *depressed*. I've read that

48

sadness isn't depression; that in depression, one is apathetic. I don't agree with this because all through what I still call *depression*, I determined to keep interested: to be alive to life. Even though mine had been changed so much without my mom, I went on. I lived on. I somehow knew I'd keep making it, even though it had become a way of life to have to. One day while I was rereading your book *What Is God Like?*, it came to me: since when was life conceived to be the height of happiness, well-being, or anything that people today insist upon? Having always been so happy, grieving still seemed utterly strange to me—foreign—unfamiliar. Only a person who has lost the one most dear could understand. Why should one, *unless*?

"But now something is changing. You see, all this time it didn't seem *real* that my mom was gone—really gone. I'd walk through the stores downtown where we'd shopped together so often, and it didn't seem real that she wasn't trotting along beside me. And believe me, it didn't help one bit that she was ninety-six years old when she died! I'd wander through the empty rooms of our house; then I'd sit in my room at night and watch the trees blow in front of the street light, and everything seemed the way it always was. What *wasn't* real was that I couldn't slip across the hall to my mom's room for a chat or a giggle about some secret thing. It didn't seem plausible that anything had changed!

"Now, after more than two years without her, at last I *know* and recognize my *aloneness*. A better word is 'apartness'. Like Alice and the Red Queen, I've crossed a brook. I'm on into the next square. Reality is all around me, and I sense in myself a new tenderness, a new awareness. (Mocking birds even sound different.)

I am essentially alone, and this is real to me. I'm not complaining. This is just—it. It's a certain peace and a sureness I never knew before. Suddenly I've almost stopped *questioning*. And whether it's a turning to go here or to go there, well, it's all right. This is a *new* place, where no new dearest love may go. How shall I say it? You're—*apart*. You're alone and you're *apart*. I tell myself it must be the *infinite loneliness* of being alone with Jesus. But after all, whose birds and trees are these? Yes, I now know and accept that I'm truly alone—apart. Still, I'm goin' great guns!"

My friend has shared one of the most definite illustrations of God's grace breaking through a long, wearing grief. There are both joy and sorrow in her words. There are tears, but also a chuckle: she's now "goin' great guns!" "I've come to a conclusion," her letter ended. "Grieving isn't going to bring my mom back. Neither is it going to do her a bit of good! Grieving is just going to deprive me of living, and I'm not ready for that. I've been slow to cross over the brook, but I've crossed over."

There is no virtue or lack of it in the time required for each of us to sort things out enough to begin to accept the ever-flowing grace of God. Some are quick to step out when He speaks; others are more cautious, more thoughtful. Of course, the depth of our grief and the *real reason* for it can slow the process, too.

Right here, I should expand a bit on what I mean by the *real reason* for a continuing grief. What I say may sound cruel on first reading, but I am trying to be not only honest, but *real*. Am I daring to suggest a probing self-analysis in the midst of a fresh grief? Certainly not. No one should attempt such an effort until he or she is honestly ready *and* rested enough to find the way out of the smothering experience of the fresh loss. Before then, any kind of introspection could only damage. Actually, as the years pass, I become more wary of most introspection. And yet in order to be honest both with God and with ourselves, a certain amount of it, objectively handled, is necessary. Naturally, when a grief is fresh—before the funeral flowers have wilted—we can't be expected to be objective. There is no way not to think about our loss. There is no such thing as "getting your mind off it". Only an abnormal mind would be able to turn off grief. A normal mind cannot shut itself off, cannot stop thinking.

But if the grieving goes on and on, we need to ask ourselves bluntly: "*Why* am I so torn up by what has happened? Is it because I loved someone else too much? Or is it because *I am lost*—certain that I will never learn how to begin my day alone? Is my grief normal? Does it continue like this because I can't seem to learn how to live half a life? Am I really grieving over my loved one—*or* am I, in fact, grieving because *I will never* be able to enjoy all those happy times again? Do I truly believe that my loved one *is* fully alive—that he or she *is* somewhere on that mysterious journey—a little way ahead of me? Perhaps I'm grieving because I can't find my loved one. We always stayed in such close contact, and now suddenly I don't know where to call him! I don't know *how* to reach her! What is he doing? What is she doing? I'm accustomed to knowing, and maybe this is causing me unbearable grief!"

Even if your self-questioning turns up guilt over what you did or did not do for your loved one, God's forgiveness covers this too. Once a loved one is gone, we all smart under what suddenly appears to have been our shortcomings while the loved one was still with us. This is only human, but we need to guard against false guilt. Your loved one wasn't a saint either! So, when you feel up to facing them, these questions can help—if they're answered honestly.

If, in the process, we find one or more of our answers loaded with self-pity, this is the place to determine our *real reason* for grieving. (There is a difference, you know, between normal grief and continual grieving. Grief is normal; but prolonged grieving is destructive not only to us, but to those around us.)

"Why," a widower wrote, "doesn't God help me? I am growing more miserable every day lived without my beloved wife. I am at the place where my pity for myself is choking me. I am a pitiful excuse for a man!" This lonely gentleman answered his own question, apparently not realizing it. *God cannot send redemptive help to anyone steeped in self-pity.*

What is God's way in human suffering? I have been exploring this question for many years now, and this is what I have found: Jesus Christ, the Redeemer, is unwilling for any grief or sorrow to be wasted. He *wants* to make creative, redemptive use of all of it—but there is a condition. He will do this (He *can* do this) *only if we permit Him to do it*. When we are torn apart by grief, it's hard—sometimes impossible—for us to know what our part is in this redemptive process which He longs to carry out in us.

"What do you mean," asked a college girl, heartbroken at the death of her mother, "when you say *if we let Him? What am I supposed to do? What can I do? How do I let God help me with my grief?"

Our part is to do all we can to keep ourselves from collapsing into that well of self-pity. It's just that simple, and it's just that difficult. Of course, if our lost loved one has spoiled us, even seeing and admitting our self-pity becomes much more difficult. If, with our loved one, we have both practised courage before each other, the task becomes easier, the incentive more certain.

Of course, no one is going to be expecting help from God if he or she has no faith in Him. Faith is presupposed here. But beyond the exercise of our faith, feeble as it may be, the only thing we need to do is to keep ourselves from saying *or* feeling that we are too precious for such a dreadful thing to have happened to us, and this is anything but easy. Pain of any kind occupies our first attention. It is *natural* to pity those in pain, and it is certainly natural to pity ourselves in pain. Merely to say that if we are Christians we have access to the *supernatural* is not enough. As Christians, we *do* have access to the Spirit of the living God, but we have to try this truth for ourselves. We can be told until our ears ring that God lives in us and that He is powerful enough to turn us around—even to change our minds—but until we try this truth in a hard place, minus self-pity, we don't really know it or own it.

I fail to see how anyone who does not believe in the Ongoing Life in Christ can live through the grief which follows death or the knowledge of a loved one's incurable illness. I have never understood that. Intellectually, I can comprehend and admire the fact of human courage, chin up, life must go on, etcetera; but in my heart I just don't understand anyone without Jesus Christ ever wanting to live after the loss of a loved one.

Until I was thirty-three years old, I believed there was nothing after death, and through every year of my teens, twenties, and into my thirties, I sometimes lived in agonizing fear of the death of my parents, my brother, or one or two other persons whose lives were a part of mine. I now know at least something of what St. Paul meant when he declared that because Jesus lives, the sting has been removed from death. In the sense of permanent separation, the sting *is* gone. Jesus promised that wherever He was, there we would be—right with Him. Now that I am His follower, I am no longer afraid—either of my own death or of a permanent separation from someone I love. I am still afraid of the pain of grief, until we're together again, but no longer do I fear the non-existent permanent separation. "He that liveth and believeth in me shall never die." I find nothing flimsy or uncertain about taking Jesus Christ at His word. For me, that much is irrevocably settled. Neither I nor my loved one will ever die.

Still, this sweeping certainty does not bring back the dear, familiar face across the room. The knowledge that our loved ones are *living* somewhere removes the sting, but it does not refill the present emptiness in our lives. Nor does it answer our inevitable questions about *why* the loss had to occur. And in spite of the title of this book, I consider our *questions* as inevitable as our grief. I should have done a wrong thing in writing this if anyone got even the faintest notion that I believe *questions* are wrong. The title is *No Pat Answers*. In no way is it implied that we should add false guilt to the pain of our grief by feeling out of harmony with God over our natural, human questions. The premise throughout every chapter is this: questions are probably going to float to the surface of our minds when our hearts break, whether we voice them or not. But to expect—or more unrealistic—to attempt to *give*—"pat answers" is demeaning to the Lord Himself.

We have all heard most of the religious clichés about God which insist that He has sent tragedy or illness. Frankly, I hadn't encountered any of these (to me) cruel "explanations" of suffering for many years. Then in one week I received three letters from persons whose normal grief had been turned into near hysteria because a well-meaning minister or saint had given one of these terrifying "pat answers".

First, a woman in her thirties had lost her only child from leukemia. The seven-year-old girl had been this widowed mother's life. "Someone at church" had told her that God *took* that child because He demanded to be at the centre of everyone's life. The mother was unconsolable. So far as I know, she is still in a mental institution.

The next letter was from a man who had lost his wife and two children in a boating accident. He also had been "advised" in a most fearful, sanity-shaking manner: his little family had been wiped out because he, the father and husband, had chosen to take his loved ones on Sunday picnics during the summer, rather than to church!

The third letter came from a young mother who had been assured that her small son's blindness as a consequence of a fireworks accident had "been visited upon the son" due to the wickedness of the father. The wound was double-edged since the boy's father had been killed the previous year in Vietnam. The only "wickedness" the grieving, distraught mother could imagine in her always faithful husband was an occasional social drink.

I admit these are extreme examples, but God is *not* like this. His ways are higher than our ways, yet being "higher" does not mean He is immune to our pain. To insist that God *takes* our loved ones in order to punish us or to prove His power to do exactly as He pleases is an insult to the great, loving God-heart which broke on Calvary.

Did Jesus come to make it possible for us to discover the real nature of the Father's heart? Was St. John wrong when he wrote that the Son of God, Jesus Christ, ". . . He hath revealed Him?" Was Jesus confused when He declared that "I and the Father are one?" How can a punishing, death-dealing God be of the same nature as Jesus Christ who walked the earth with healing in His hands? Who ultimately, *willingly* offered those hands to be nailed to the cross for love's sake?

God doesn't want any human being's place in our lives. He wants His own place. Only He is God.

He did not want the mother whose child died of leukemia to love the child less. God has put the cure for leukemia in the world, and one day man will find it, as he has found the means of preventing polio.

And do you really think that the Lord decided that killing off a man's family would make a churchgoer of him?

Did God plan the Vietnam War and the firecracker session which widowed the young mother and blinded her little boy?

Where do you think such ideas came from in the first place? An anthropologist could explain, I suppose. That they *are* primitive ideas, no one could deny. And I am using the word *primitive* in its strictest sense. Ancient man believed that he had to placate his gods. He believed that every good or bad event in his life could be laid directly to an act of the gods.

I am aware that many of you may be quoting these courageous words of the suffering Job as you read: ". . . the Lord gave, and the Lord has taken away; blessed be the name of the Lord." Do I think Job was wrong? Am I challenging the Scriptures? Neither. But if man had been sufficiently enlightened to have lived the "abundant life" during Job's time, *before* Jesus came, *before* the New Testament—if man had had sufficient knowledge of the free gift of salvation *then*—why did Jesus have to come?

If it helps you in your grief to believe literally that "the Lord takes away . . .", by all means, believe it! In the first pages of this book I said that I was willing and prepared to be misunderstood and that I had no intention of disturbing anyone's faith—*if* he or she has no problems with the questions raised here.

I do have problems with them. In short, I am a Christian because I am convinced that only *in* Jesus Himself is there any adequate, calming, useful, *clear* explanation of any of life's tragedies. We dare not isolate one or two verses of Scripture and fling them about when the heart breaks. If a "taking" God was truly revealed in Jesus Christ, then why did Jesus weep at death? Indeed, why did He raise people from the dead? Job's brave, faith-filled line helps me too, but *only* when I read it in the context of the life of the Saviour, who alone has removed death's sting. The Saviour who surely has *earned* the right to say to us at the open graves of our loved ones: "Let not your hearts be troubled. ..." The Saviour who has been there and back safely, who died and rose again and now can fully assure us.

Some Eastern religions still hold to the theory that man gets what he deserves. If this were God's intent, we'd all be sunk. I certainly cringe at the idea of getting what I deserve from God. To say a loved one died because of some sin in our lives is not only unrealistic, distorted thinking for a Christian, in whom "the light of the world" *lives*, but is an insult to the forgiving heart of the Father.

When my heart is burdened down with grief, I am lifted up and sustained by the sure knowledge that God *receives* my loved one who, according to his own understanding, has said—or even thought: "Lord, I believe. Help thou mine unbelief." God is "not willing that any should perish". The daily life of Jesus, as we find it in the gospels, substantiates this for me. And more than His daily life—His sacrificial death.

My *human spirit* is challenged by Job's awesome courage. When a man can sit in the midst of misery such as his and declare: "The Lord gave, and the Lord has taken away; blessed be the name of the Lord," then I have to be inspired by his faith and his open, childlike heart. I have not come to any definite conclusion concerning this matter, but I wonder if perhaps a deeper meaning to Job's word could be something like this: I have no answer to why this series of blows has fallen on me. Because "I know that my redeemer liveth", I will seek no answer. My friends are all trying to give me pat answers, but I refuse to listen. I reject both blame and blamelessness. *I cling only to God.*

Job's friends came, expounding their pat answers, but Job clung to his confidence in the character of the Lord he followed. He refused either to judge God or to be judged himself by what had happened.

Plato has been called "a Christian born out of due time". I have always thought of Job in that way. The grace of Jesus Christ had not yet been loosed in the world, but Job conducted himself with more grace than most of us show as we go pattering about expounding our superficial explanations.

The grief which follows the death of a loved one is not the only kind of grief we suffer. Back in the seventeenth century the Italian poet Pietro Metastasio wrote: "If the internal griefs of every man could be read, written on his forehead, how many who now excite envy would appear to be objects of pity?" How many indeed?

We all carry internal griefs, some dimmed by the years or by our refusal to listen to a certain piece of music, but old griefs remain, hidden for the most part, their edges duller by new jobs or new places. Still, the scars are there, and at times we can only hope they are hidden. Disappointment, disillusionment, and failure can be sources of real grief, but the conclusion must be the same: There are no pat answers to the handling of these seemingly lesser griefs. Perhaps, in reality, they are not smaller than the grief which follows the loss of a loved one, since there is a certain finality about death—a definite place to try to begin again. In the long run, the "internal griefs" may be harder to endure, especially if for some reason we feel they have to be kept secret.

In the small community where I live there are several divorcees whose husbands have found other women at a time when their marriages should have been in full

59

bloom. These grieving women cannot share their grief openly as one can share the sorrow of death. Others may sympathize with them, but find it embarrassing or in bad taste to express their sympathy. These women whose husbands have found someone else feel, I'm sure, that somewhere *they* must have failed. And so along with the grief of losing their loved one, they carry a kind of double load of shame and guilt which forces them to smile, play endless hands of bridge, join clubs, and go out to dinner together in an effort to stay off the subject—to keep the grief hidden. This kind of pain has no abrupt finality, for there is no grave to leave. Where does one begin again?

I find no end to the list of human griefs. For years I heard regularly from a lady whose only son was in prison for life. I tried, but I really could not imagine the weight of her hidden grief. Finally, in his fifties, the son died while still in prison. The last time I heard from her, she told me that somehow she feels freed now. In one way, the awful finality of death is its ugliest aspect; in another way, it is the saving factor.

Philosophers have wrestled with this problem of suffering through grief for as long as there have been philosophers. Jesus walked straight into the midst of this philosophical turmoil. He walked in and declared that tribulation of all kinds is to be expected in this life. Then He said: "Follow me" *through* it. That would seem to end the turmoil and the confusion, but it hasn't. And only those who are willing to think it through realistically, in the presence of the One who has lived through both grief *and* death, can come to accept the suffering without bitterness.

Chapter 5

Watching Our Loved Ones Suffer

I doubt that there is any mental torture comparable to watching our loved ones suffer, especially when there is little or nothing we can do to help them.

In *What Is God Like?*, my favourite among all my earlier books, I have written at length about my own ordeal as, along with my mother and brother, I stood by and watched my father slowly die of leukemia. We all knew he was dying; he didn't know, and the three of us had decided not to tell him. My father's nature was happy and buoyant, really almost childlike; we all felt that his confidence that he could get well just might help bring about the miracle. Week after week he endured the needle in his veins, while hour after crawling hour the blood of his many friends dripped into his body to keep him alive. His bone marrow had been almost entirely replaced by leukemia cells, and although he was conscious until the end, there was never any real hope. After all these years we still have not stopped missing him, but the night he died, we thanked God that he was free of his pitiful ordeal.

I learned much during those days of watching my gentle father, who had never been ill, find his own way through his suffering. He was magnificent! I, who had always been proud of him, had never been so proud. His childlike confidence in Jesus Christ, from the moment of his conversion just a few years before his illness to the moment of his death, is still strengthening my confidence.

Watching my mother's courage in the midst of her suffering during those months was equally as difficult for me—especially during the hard days when she was confined to her bed with a painful back injury and could not visit Dad at the hospital. She suffered both mental and physical anguish.

During one of his brief stays at home, Dad had gallantly tried to get to the breakfast table to eat with Mother and watch the birds at the feeders. This had been the morning routine for almost all the years of their married life. To have a breakfast at the table with her again, to see those birds, suddenly became terribly important to him. Mother pushed him to the table in the wheelchair, and as he struggled to lift himself from the chair in order to sit "like always" in his favourite place, he fainted, fell directly on Mother, and caused a serious muscle tear in her back.

What seemed to sustain her during those days when she was confined to her bed was the fact that she had managed to keep my father's head from striking the wrought iron corner of the kitchen table.

Strange, small things like this help us through our own suffering. Perhaps even our questions help too. I soon gave up trying to convince Mother to stop her daily puzzling about how such a dreadful disease as leukemia could strike my father who had always been in excellent health. She went over and over their carefully planned menus. Mother is a marvellous cook, and I have no memories of poorly planned, unnourishing meals at home. "He always had lots of rare beef and steak," she would repeat. "I could never get him to eat liver, but I saw to it that he compensated in other ways." My mother is an intelligent woman, widely read on medical and scientific facts. She knew perfectly well that my father's fatal disease was *not* caused by a faulty diet. Even if he had eaten unbalanced meals, there was no medical evidence that this could have affected the situation one way or another. The only theory (and it was just a theory) which anyone set forth was that perhaps as a dentist he had over-exposed himself to dental X-ray through the years. Even now, Mother will sometimes repeat her little routine about how strange it was that such a healthy, well-fed man could contract leukemia. Occasionally I try to change the subject, but only occasionally because she is a woman with a healthy mind and healthy emotions and has never kept her grief alive by dwelling on these thoughts.

Her questions helped her during those days while we waited, though. They occupied her thoughts and gave her a puzzle to solve. I could see the relief it brought her, even though—and this is my point—her words tore through *me* like knives. My father and I were very much alike in appearance and emotions. When something affected us deeply, we *couldn't* talk about it. I still can't, but it helps Mother, and I believe this is one of the secrets of watching a loved one suffer: to direct our own attention to another person in need.

If you walk a hospital corridor alone, as I have done three times within the past two years, there's no problem finding another lone watcher to attend, even in a small way. I remember one poor lady who had stayed around the clock for five days with her dying husband. When we met in the hospital corridor, I tried to be pleasant in order to encourage her, but she helped *me* so much one day by the simplest question imaginable. She smiled a little and said, "Your feet get to hurtin', don't they—after awhile?" My feet did hurt, and it helped that she knew.

I watched my mother endure intense physical pain after she fell last year and broke her leg. My own suffering was eased, though, because my dear friend Nancy Goshorn watched with me. Nancy and her aunt, Mother's neighbours, had managed to get my mother to the hospital in an ambulance the night she fell in her own kitchen—staying in off the icy sidewalks "because I don't want to take any chances of falling right now when Genie's working so hard to meet her deadline on *Lighthouse*". Nancy and my brother were with her for the surgery, and then there was only Nancy until I could collect the final pages of my manuscript and hop a plane. I finished marking the pages at the hospital while I watched by Mother's bed. But this was a different kind of watching. Mother was in agonizing pain, especially when she had to try those first laboured steps with the walker, but she wasn't going to die. I knew that, and there was Nancy's unbelievable love and devotion, which sustained *me* far more than Nancy believes.

Each time of watching is different. Our questions can vary all the way from "Why did this have to happen now?" to "What next?" Occasionally we even find ourselves able to laugh because laughter and humour are among God's greatest relaxers. But there is nothing harder to bear than watching the pain of a loved one while we stand by helplessly.

64

My best friend at Ohio University was a fun-loving, dark-eyed teenager named Eleanor. We weren't much alike, but we were "best friends" then, and the years have not changed our friendship in spite of infrequent visits. Aside from having learned a lot of the right and wrong things together when we were kooky college kids, both of us have always loved writing. Eleanor has been a successful newspaper woman since her graduation from the university, and she is doing a marvellous job as an editor for the *Miami Herald* and as the author of the widely read advice feature called "Column With a Heart", which she writes under the name of Eleanor Hart.

Over a year ago, another college friend told me she had heard that Eleanor's beautiful and talented daughter, Mary, had been in a coma for months in Florida hospital. Eleanor and I don't write often, so I knew nothing of this. In answer to my airmail letter, I received the following clipping from the *Miami Herald*—Eleanor's column for 9th August, 1970—reprinted here with her permission.

WITH GOD NOTHING
SHALL BE IMPOSSIBLE

Dear Readers:

A hospital is another world, its heartbreak and hope unknown to the mainstream of society until . . . until tragedy catapults a loved one into its Twilight Zone. Only then does the agony of human suffering, which hospital personnel live with every day, come alive for the complacent in that other world of regulated conformity.

Yet, miraculously, human beings do have a "fail-safe" system that enables them to live with misery. How many times has it been said, and exemplified, "God does not send a cross heavier than one can bear?"

Today's letter is from a mother whose daughter has been on the critical list for more than a month following brain surgery.

Eleanor Hart

Dear Eleanor Hart:

Strange as it seems, one can learn to live with agony—agony of a devastatingly sick dear one who hovers not only on the brink of physical recovery, but of mental awareness.

God knows I am not alone. There are thousands who have, and who are, living with a similar nightmare ... the nightmare of looking at a beautiful young person prone, a tube in her throat, her right arm stilled by paralysis, the sweet little girl face once so mobile, now immobile.

And the eyes, my God, the eyes—those enormous pools of amber sadness that seem to look right through you, then turn away.

"It's Mother and Daddy," my husband and I chorus hopefully at her bedside. "Hello, darling. We love you so much. You look beautiful. You're doing fine, May-May (her pet name as a child). You're going to get better, we just know it."

Sometimes the left corner of the mouth tilts slightly, then the eyes shift—left, then right.

"I think she knows us," my husband theorizes comfortingly. "Any day now, there'll be a breakthrough."

I echo his hope orally, but in my thoughts the horror stalks, unrelentingly. . . . Will we ever again hear her say in that sweet, gentle voice, "Mother and Daddy"?

Oh, God, what I wouldn't give to hear her say, "Oh, Mother!" in the tone of exasperation she always used when we disagreed about some trifle.

I say "trifle" because any grief I thought I'd ever known is just that.

Thoughts multiply into a mirage of torment:

Why can't God take my life and resurrect her? Why should I, at middle-age, be in good health while my darling, less than half my years, lies there, an inert form with only a ghost of life?

It does no good to go to bed and pray never to awaken. That would be too simple, and who would benefit? Only I.

No dawn breaks eternally, and gradually, mercifully, I am learning to live with the horror—not only the agony of her suffering, but of not knowing what the outcome will be.

Yet, my husband and I are fortunate. We have each other, and somehow the burden of interminable anguish is less when two people bear it together.

"I know she's going to make it, honey," he says softly, and the look in his amber eyes, so like hers, has a warmth that reaches out and enfolds me.

Numbly, I turn away, fighting, fighting, fighting to stem the tidal wall of tears, and reminding, oh reminding myself a thousand times of the words from St. Luke:

"For with God, nothing shall be impossible."

Signed—Living in Hope

My friend didn't have to tell me that she, the columnist, had written both the editor's note *and* the letter. I recognized her poignant, readable style, but I also recognized her writer's need to attempt to ease her own heart's pain a little by putting some of it down in words. This helps those of us who write for a living, and it helps anyone in anguish of any kind. Some relief is bound to come from pouring it out, but I'm also certain that Eleanor strengthened her faith by reminding herself that "God does not send a cross heavier than one can bear" and that ". . . with God, nothing shall be impossible".

I learned later that she had been forced to write anonymously, as though she were a reader, because her rest had been disturbed so often by well-meaning but insensitive persons from a variety of religious sects who insisted upon calling or catching her in the hospital corridors to urge upon her and her heartbroken husband their special "healing" prayers. "We appreciated their interest, certainly," she told me during a recent visit in my home. "But most of those people made me feel creepy—as though they might try to get me down on my knees right there in public. I had a funny feeling that their insistence in the face of our obvious grief and exhaustion somehow had more to do with their egos than with Mary's getting well!"

The end of Eleanor's story will be told in the next chapter since this chapter concerns the agony of watching loved ones suffer. I've had some experience with it myself, but I doubt that I would have dared write this chapter had Eleanor and Noel Ratelle not shared with me at least something of the horror through which they lived. And they did live through it; in less than a year from the date of that column, I spent a genuinely happy day with them. Eleanor's face still mirrors the deep suffering, but her mind is seemingly free of bitterness. Neither she nor Noel ever brings up their shared tragedy, but they speak of Mary naturally. Our conversation about their painful watching period—six long months—was my idea. I wanted to be able to handle this chapter with authenticity because some of you may be going through the same kind of debilitating anguish.

The watching period, when you can do nothing, it seems, but watch and wait and wonder in your heart what God's part in it really is. How He will get you through it. You wonder in your heart and try, *try* in your own way and according to your understanding to handle the questions which will almost surely come.

Do we dare confront those suffering through a watching period with the *fact of Jesus Christ*? If we know Him as He really is, yes. We will not deepen their bruises by speaking of Jesus because He is the One about whom Isaiah wrote, "A bruised reed shall he not break, and the smoking flax shall he not quench. . . ."

Those who "barge in" upon human suffering may come in the "name of Jesus", but certainly they do not come in His *nature*.

Jesus never forces entrance, never insists. He waits. No one could understand the agony of waiting, of watching as He understands it. He always moves within an aura of gentle, firm, enlightened tenderness, experienced as He is with watching His loved ones suffer without Him—without knowing that He is there—waiting.

So, I have written this chapter, feeling that Eleanor and Noel Ratelle would agree that Jesus Christ waits with us as we watch our loved ones suffer. And with joy and gratitude I have dedicated this book to them.

Chapter 6

Too Young To Die

Some time in the first half of the nineteenth century, the American journalist Nathaniel Willis wrote: "Youth is beautiful. Its friendship is precious. The intercourse with it is a purifying release from the worn and stained hardness of older life." Mr. Willis "penned his tribute" to youth about the same time the English poet Joseph Ridgeway wrote these early Victorian lines: "Youth is the gay and pleasant spring of life, when joy is stirring in the dancing blood, and nature calls us with a thousand songs to share her general feast."

Recently at an autographing party, I thought one mother might lose her poise entirely when I greeted her teen-aged son with: "Hey, I like your hair!" The well-groomed lady was obviously embarrassed because her son's clean, slightly wavy hair hung to his shoulders. Her face was as red as his faded red corduroy pants. I did like his hair. And his open, smilingly handsome face (fringed, of course, with what he could muster in the way of a beard) made me happy just to look at him. He wasn't a hippie or a drug addict or a freak. He was just the age he was, and his mother was the age she was. She was self-conscious—he was disarmingly unself-conscious. "Joy (was) stirring in (his) dancing blood, and nature (was calling) . . . with a thousand songs to share her general feast."

When I came upon the above lines, written more than a century ago, I thought of this young man. There he stood—not swaggering, not blushing, not shifting from one foot to the other—just *waiting* for all of life. Then I searched until I found the quotation from Willis because my brief meeting with the lad had quite unexpectedly given *me* "... a purifying release from the worn and stained hardness of older life". He didn't scowl when his mother's discomfort over his appearance showed so plainly. He smiled, and, quite frankly, I needed his smile and found his mother's humiliation pathetic.

I've thought about him since and wished him well in what I hope is a long, long life. In one sense my future is in his hands and in the hands of other young men like him, some with even longer hair and less open faces. A few moments conversation had assured me that this Adonis with the swinging, red-gold wavy hair held concerns about life that mattered. He spoke easily of love—the love of God—and how we'd better "get with" sharing that love.

How a young man wears his hair could not be less important. How a young woman wears her hair doesn't matter either. What matters when you are young is that you are permitted *to live*—to be here, ready to respond to the "thousand songs" that call you to "the general feast".

Don't misunderstand. The young do not go around fearing death. They fear man's destruction of the earth on which God has set him; they see the futility of man's favourite game of war. But they don't fear dying. Death isn't real to them. In fact, they seem to love macabre events, books, movies, plays. But even though I can't prove this, I just don't believe the young think much about their own deaths. It's too far removed from the exuberance of *today*.

A few years ago I watched the faces of six pallbearers, none over eighteen, as they carried the body of a member of their school football team to his grave. The six youthful bearers were solemn. They would miss their friend. But I got the feeling that the tragedy affected us adults far more deeply. This does not indicate hardness in the young; it indicates age in us. We know something of what the dead boy missed by never being alive on this earth in his twenties or forties or fifties. I believe that nothing sends a chill through the heart of an adult more quickly than the sudden death of the very young.

To millions and millions of adults, from the beginning of so-called civilized history, this quick, unacceptable chill has come. We resist the chopping off, the life not lived, the chance lost forever to succeed or fail, to love or destroy. Even if a life is lived poorly, there is something in us which declares it should have a chance.

Not long ago I had lunch with two friends from the publishing world. One of them, a sensitive, caring man in his mid-fifties, was discussing the book he was currently reading: *The Winds of War*, Herman Wouk's best-selling novel about World War II. My friend is an astute man, a sophisticated man, not given to saying the obvious. The book had whisked him back over the years in his own memory to the strange, frightening period of his life as an ambulance driver during that war. His face creased with sudden sorrow. "I can still see some of those bleeding young men we picked up," he said,

73

almost to himself. "This book has made me remember them. I wonder which of them lived and which of them died." I could almost see the chill pass through him as he added, almost naïvely: "It's even more horrible to me now that I'm older! Do you know how *young* they all were?"

Too young to die.

In the preceding chapter, I wrote of the long, seemingly endless waiting period through which my college friend, Eleanor Ratelle, and her husband, Noel, watched their young daughter lie in a coma. My friends' waiting and watching finally ended: Mary died on a Christmas morning. Here is an excerpt from the letter I received at the time.

Dear Genie,

Thank you for writing again to ask. The enclosed clipping tells the tale. It's all over. My beautiful baby is at rest.

I am glad she died because she couldn't get better. But as to why she was stricken, well, that's something else. Malformation of the veins and arteries, the death certificate reads. But what caused it? The neurosurgeons who operated on her can tell us nothing. I will have to find a way to stop repeating my question, and I will. . . .

You are right. There are no pat answers! I'm glad you'll write that book. All I know is that some of us make it and can live awhile and some of us don't. I do know the goodness of your life here on earth has nothing to do with it. Mary was an angel in life. . . .

People keep saying to me, "How can you stand it?

How can you stand it? How will you and Noel live without her?"

Honestly, the things people say! But maybe they need to ask these questions. Maybe it helps them to ask. I simply reply that you either lie down or stand up and that I'm not ready to lie down—yet. My favourite retort when people say in a quavering voice: "Eleanor, how are you?" is just this—"I'm walking around."

And, dear Genie, so I am.

Much, much love,
Eleanor

The Ratelles believe in Jesus Christ, but this letter was written during those first vacuous days following the tragedy, and Eleanor is far too real to have written any "spiritual-sounding" platitudes which she didn't feel at that moment. She knew that I knew that only God can hold a human heart through an ordeal such as hers. Only faith in His ultimate goodness could hold back the perfectly understandable urge she had "to pray never to awaken". People in Eleanor's dilemma have committed suicide. She didn't, but neither did she preach me a sermon or quote any Scripture in that letter telling me that Mary was dead.

She did state her question though. "What caused it?" And to me this is the normal question. Any *parent* would long to have some sort of explanation from the doctors who had operated on the child. Apparently there was no answer. But Eleanor's question was *not*, if you notice, directed at God. She has not, so far as I know, shouted at the heavens for an answer—a pat, understandable answer in human terms—as to why *her* daughter had to die. Is this a sign of deep, abiding faith even under circumstances like these? I don't know. I'm fairly certain my realistic, courageous friend hasn't given the grandeur of her own faith a thought. I'm even more convinced that if I brought it up she would simply tilt her head to one side, look away for a minute in her characteristic fashion, and reply: "I don't go around trying to measure my own faith. I just keep going."

People prayed for Mary's physical healing. Wasn't God listening? Why did this capable, attractive young woman have to die at twenty-six?

If Eleanor and Noel Ratelle have asked this question of God, they have not allowed the fact that they have received *no pat answer* to embitter their lives. One year later, they're both excellent company. I look forward to their visits not only because I enjoy them so much, but because I need to learn from them. Our talk now moves on far more serious levels than it might have two years ago, but it moves. These middle-aged, lovable, heart-broken people are *alive*. They haven't given up in any way. They don't belabour the subject of their daughter's death. When I ask a question, their replies are thoughtful, natural, and free from bitterness. They do not pity themselves because this hideous thing happened to them.

Neither articulates faith as some of us do, but both show all the practical, deep-down indications that Someone is holding them very, very steady. You know how difficult it usually is just to be *with* friends who have suffered as these two suffered so recently. Not so with them. They are going on with life.

Call it providence or coincidence, but I recently learned of a woman who must now go on alone because her husband—unable to endure the grief—took his own life when word came that their only son had been killed in Vietnam. It was a selfish act, of course; he managed to double his wife's sorrow. But it is never a mystery to me when anyone fails in trying to face tragedies *without some sense of God*.

To me, the mystery is the courage and faith in Life Himself, as shown by my friends the Ratelles. This is a mystery because it is of God, and He refuses to hamper us with "pat answers". Frail, weak, cowardly human behaviour I can undestand, if I take time to think, but we waste our time and our efforts when we try to limit God to our concept of what *is* loving care from Him and what is *not*. There is no way for us to understand *why* the young die. They do, as we do. Long ago we should have stopped trying to recreate God into our image. Anyone can know the heart and intent of God because Jesus Christ has made that clear, but His reasons for allowing death, violence, and suffering in the world He created are a *mystery*. It is only conceit and futility to attempt to understand or explain.

The Psalmist told us to ". . . be of good courage." Courage is required, and our courage in times of tragedy does not diminish God. Nowhere does God promise immunity from deep sorrow, but He did say, ". . . I am with you always." *Not* that He would make us feel "just fine" in a minute, but that He would be *with us*.

Probably we won't feel fine for a long time, but He will be with us, and we *can* go on "walking around".

Chapter 7

Too Old To Live

In an earlier chapter I shared with you the experience of my friend Frances during her own pilgrimage out of the destructiveness and depression of grief after the death of her mother. Recently Frances spent her vacation on the Island where I live, and one night I discussed this chapter with her because I value her reactions. As we talked, her eyes brightened and she perched on the edge of her chair with near delight at the realization that her mother had not had to experience the futility of the helpless aged who lie in nursing homes across the world. When she was almost ninety-six, Tessie Pitts, still attractive and active, died of pneumonia. She had never spent a night in a nursing home and only a relatively few nights in a hospital. She had been able to live out her long life in her own home among her own family. In fact, when Tessie Pitts died, she really seemed to be "too young to die".

But she was a rare exception. What of the thousands upon thousands of elderly people who, when they are lucid, spend these few hours wondering—perhaps even crying out for the answer—why they *can't* die?

A saintly elderly missionary named Maria Frederickson became my close and dear friend a few years before she died. When I first met the octogenarian Maria, she was vigorous, spry, and vitally interested in life. She showered me with provocative, love-filled letters, and instead of pouting, as her age might have allowed, if I didn't answer at once, she never failed to show surprise and pleasure when I finally got around to a reply. Occasionally she sent me a present, and as she had little money, her gifts were always from among her lifetime collection of treasures: a coin from Damascus—"like on the headdress of the woman in the parable of the lost coin", a beautiful pin, a hand-blown blue glass bowl from the Holy Land, a delicately embroidered satin Chinese jacket; and the last time I visited her in the convalescent home, she gave me a picture of herself when she was young and pretty, mounted in an old bird's-eye maple frame. I loved Maria, and I learned from her. But I also watched her live through a few ghastly years.

The nursing home where she shared a room was as good as most modest institutions of its kind—understaffed, of course, but almost always reasonably clean. At least the harried personnel did their best, Maria said, to keep the beds changed.

Maria was alert to the end, and sometimes I wished she hadn't been—especially during the visit when she told me of her terror the night before when an elderly woman down the hall had crept into her room and tried to jerk off Maria's nightgown, scratching and clawing in the process. "She thought it was *her* nightgown," Maria explained. "Almost nobody here is in his right mind, Genie. I'm not complaining. I've lost interest in food, so that part's all right. They keep me clean, and now and then someone I love like you pays me a visit. I'd have no problems at all, if only the others here were in their right minds. I ask God to keep back my fear, but I'm afraid of some of them."

Of course, there are sociological explanations for the inadequacy of our care of the aged and ill. You've read, as I have, that state mental institutions are so over-crowded that often their aged overflow is sent to area convalescent homes. This is true, I know, in the more modest homes such as Maria's. I've visited others where friends have been genuinely contented. But these were authentic retirement homes, far more expensive, and normally application for entrance must be made years in advance.

Having no children to burden with my own old age, I certainly plan to think well in advance on the subject of a retirement home, providing I keep my mental acumen. But often this is not possible. Anyway, I imagine most of us kid ourselves into believing that we'll just suddenly keel over with a convenient heart attack someday at the appropriate time and that will be that. A nice idea, but it doesn't always happen that way. People grow old and then older and more helpless, and for convenience sake or because there is no way to care for even their most basic needs, they are put into a nursing home.

"It broke my heart," a woman wrote, "to have to put Mother in a home, but I have to work to support us both, and we don't have anyone but ourselves to depend on. Mother's old and ill, and I couldn't just leave her alone at home all day—bedfast!"

I have two friends who have experienced this same predicament. One made herself ill by driving hundreds of miles each weekend to sit by her elderly mother's bed in the nicest home she could find for her. My friend is free of her burden now, and so is her mother, but the other woman is still making that long, long drive—with no life of her own outside her profession. It isn't always lack of love or neglect or hardness of heart on the part of the family when they can no longer care for the elderly, helpless member.

Why do people have to keep on living? Repeatedly we hear normal, rational persons say: "I pray every day that God will take me before I am a burden on other people. I just couldn't bear that!" I've heard my own mother say this many times. I certainly understand the prayer, and I'm sure God does, but it raises more questions than anyone has ever been able to answer.

When someone does die before becoming a burden to himself and to his loved ones, does this mean God answered that person's prayer? Maria Frederickson prayed every day for years that God would let her go home before that happened, but she didn't. Why did this gentle, loving Christian lady have to live so long? I don't know. There is no pat answer to that one either. We need to be freed from the disillusionment, disappointment, and perplexity which almost inevitably follow when we *expect* God to do a certain thing under a certain set of circumstances—especially when we expect Him to act in a way which *we* can understand as being "merciful and right", as coming from the hand of *our* concept of a loving Father.

I know an elderly minister, a loyal man of God, who is pathetically puzzled now as to why God doesn't let him die and go to heaven. "I've had one stroke. I'm retired. I'm no good to the Lord anymore. I just don't understand it."

This dear man *expects* some kind of answer. Most of us do. And it doesn't come.

An acquaintance of mine writes a daily column for the *Atlanta Constitution* (my main reason for subscribing). Her name is well known; she is Celestine Sibley. I value her pieces so highly that by now the choicest compliment I can pay her is to say: "Have you read Celestine today? This one is a real *Sibley*!"

I've been saving a "real Sibley" for this chapter. The column is headlined: *God's Gift of Life*, but it isn't a paean of praise as one might expect. It is a "real Sibley"—unadorned, honest, full of both depth and perplexity—and reality.

... I guess most of us spend a lot of time wondering why God's arrangements for His world don't jibe more completely with ours. The saddest questioning came to me the other day from an 89-year-old woman who is an invalid in a local nursing home.

"I've stopped believing in God ... I think," she remarked to me as I passed her bed on the way to visit an old friend. I paused and said tentatively, "You have?"

"Sure have," she said. "Look at me—a vegetable. Only member of my family left in this world. Everybody I love has gone. Most of the time I'm not even conscious."

Her voice seemed strong and rational for that and I mentioned it.

She laughed a faint, tinny, unmirthful laugh.

"This is what they call one of my 'good days'," she said. 'That means I'm conscious ... almost. Conscious!" She said the word jeeringly and laughed again. "Is that all I'm ever going to have on my best days?"

It was a terrible question to be conscious in that place with illness and helplessness all around her couldn't be such a joyful state. Tubes went into her arm. She hadn't eaten a real meal in months. The small body under the counterpane couldn't have weighted more than 80 or 90 pounds.

She couldn't get out of bed, even to go to the bathroom. But the eyes were bright and knowledgeable and hungry with the desire to talk.

She said she had been a devout churchgoer all her life and a personal believer in God's eye-on-the-sparrow attention to His world. Then she lost a son and a daughter in an automobile accident, a bit later her husband died, and then one by one all her other relatives. She told me to look around the other beds in her ward and see if I saw a single person who "deserved" the magical, suspenseful, harrowing, horrible, happy gift of life. Few of them could see, feel, or know a thing, she said. They were an unending task for younger, stronger people who should be devoting their energies to something better.

"Why live if you don't even *know* it?" she demanded.

I fumbled for an answer—maybe a bit of Scripture that would say it for me—but the old blue eyes were fixed on me with an expression of derision.

"Get me an answer from somebody who knows," she directed imperiously. "No preachers. They're like you. They haven't been here. Ask somebody old and helpless if they're glad to be alive? Ask them to send me word *how*!"

So far I haven't got the word for her. Being old apparently isn't the problem. It's being helpless that confuses and confounds believers about a divine Plan.

Celestine Sibley is an honest writer. She hasn't "got the word" for the exhausted old lady, and because she is a realist and doesn't expect answers to every human question, Celestine isn't embarrassed not to have the answer.

But what did God mean when He said: "Before you call, I will answer"?

I don't know what He meant. At least, I don't know that He meant anything which anyone could put into words. The helpless lady who stopped Celestine Sibley was honest, too. She admitted that she no longer believed in a God who "attends" to sparrows but lets old bodies lie all but lifeless under nursing home sheets. Do you think from reading this account that the embittered, honest old woman lost her faith because God didn't prevent her children's death in that automobile? Because she lost her husband and then everyone else in her family? It would seem that she did lose it for all those reasons. To her, His eye simply must *not* be on the sparrows of this world.

But believing that God watches over and protects and shields us from harm is no reason at all to believe in Him, is it?

Would you go on believing if tragedy suddenly split your world apart? *Did* you go on believing when that happened to you? If so, then you must be close to the real reason for faith: God Himself—*not* what does or does not happen to us.

Do I have an answer to why "God permits" some people to be killed and others to escape? No. Do I have an answer to why "God permits" certain babies to be physically deformed or mentally retarded? No. Do I have an answer to why "God permitted" Eleanor's daughter to die—or Maria to live? No.

Now, will you notice that each time I mentioned "God permits", I put the words within quotation marks? Why? Don't I believe God has a permissive will? Yes. We wouldn't be here at all if He didn't. But that permissive will "permits" sin, too. Do we shout questions at the sky about sin? Some do, perhaps, but most of us, if we are truthful, must admit that the majority of the questions we fling at God have to do with some form of human suffering. We are not about to explore the relationship between sin and suffering. That is not the reason for this book. And anyway, no one has yet found an answer which resolves the question of that relationship—not to my satisfaction anyway. *Our purpose is to face up to the fact that in all of life with God, there is an area of mystery which we will never be able to understand or solve—at least in this life.*

Our purpose is extremely simple: to face our need to become realistic, so as to avoid the added, unnecessary heartache of trying to force answers which simply aren't there. In the final chapter, I hope to clarify the *one creative response* God expects from all of us. As I said in the beginning, and repeat here only to prevent some needless despair, the last chapter will hold the *key*.

I once read that if we remain healthy and live in cheerful surroundings and are ourselves cheerful, we stay "young", no matter how we must count our years. One of my dearest, closest friends who lives alone in her little cottage near my house simply *has* to be approaching one hundred years. She won't admit it because she doesn't feel old enough yet to begin boasting about her age. Oh, she remarks now and then that she wishes I had come to the Island before she had slowed down so she could have taken me on long hikes in the woods. I laugh and inform her that it's probably a good thing I came no earlier; I could never have kept up with her! Her mind is as sharp as any mind I have ever encountered, and she has lived her life so totally for other people that she just isn't interested in noticing herself enough for self-pity. I sense disappointment in her in only one way: she *has* slowed down in her body. Oh, she still keeps her own house, does her own laundry, cooks for herself, bathes herself, and shampoos her own hair, but she's disappointed and rather disgusted that these tasks now take so long.

Each time I drive away from her house, I ask myself: "What will I ever do without her? What will I do when the old body and the merry, blue eyes are out of my sight and reach?" And if she lives on to be ill and changed and helpless, I'll be lost. Lost without her and agonizing with her, because her capacity for life and fun and enjoyment is limitless. The question rises in my heart about her—the question and the prayer that she will just slip away someday to be with Jesus and not have to know one helpless hour. God may not answer that prayer—*my way*. So, you see, I'm attempting to learn from this book as I write it.

One thing is certain—the question, the ancient question, voiced so plaintively by Celestine Sibley's helpless friend in the nursing home: "Why live if you don't even know it?" *is* unanswerable in mere words.

But God. . . .

Chapter 8

The Handicapped

I thought a long time before I decided to include this chapter, and I think I hesitated because the handicapped, of all people, have enormous right to question God.

I'm beginning it now, suddenly, with a fresh sense of certainty. Why? Evidently working through this book is helping me too. I'm learning. The questions are going to come. The "pat answers" won't, but why dodge the questions? Because I am not physically handicapped is no reason to duck. After all, I hope I'm pointedly calling attention to the danger of attempting "pat answers" in response to *any* question about *any* human misfortune.

A friend, kind enough to read some of this manuscript even before it was finished, said: "I'm excited about it. Every page is as honest as pain."

I thought about her remark as I began to write this chapter. Could I continue to be as "honest as pain" and write only about the handicapped themselves? What of those whose responsibility they are? What of the mothers of cerebral palsied children? The parents of sightless, deaf, crippled, or retarded children? What questions do they fling at God—alone at night—in their beds at last? Do they ask Him, as someone asked Jesus when He healed the blind boy, whose fault it is that this child is handicapped? Why is my child blind or deaf or palsied? Is it my fault? Have I failed somewhere in what I had to give to this child genetically? Am I being punished for something I could or could not have helped. Do I *over* help my child with his handicap? Will I ever learn to live with the dread of what is going to happen to my child if I die first? *Will I ever be really rested inside?*

One such mother said to me: "Some days I just get so tired that I think I'd give ten years off my life for a week *away* from this precious, constant, frightening responsibility of caring for my son every minute." And then she laughed a little. "Of course, you know that if I ever got that chance, I couldn't and wouldn't take it! I'd be even more tired wondering if Bob is all right."

All of these questions and confusing reactions are valid. God thoroughly understands them; He knows how to take them. He knows exactly what they mean and what they do not mean. And from observation, I'd say He gives adequate grace every day to those whose responsibility it is to care for a handicapped loved one. Each person in each individual circumstance must be willing to accept that grace, and it seems that many do—willingly, gladly. Most parents, wives, husbands, brothers, sisters—even friends—whose lives revolve around the needs of an incapacitated loved one appear to make the most of being so needed. Their cheerful hourly gifts to their charges are hourly gifts to God, too.

Still, it is normal for them to question—even to doubt. And it is wrong to add false guilt to their already burdened hearts. Their burdens are as heavy as the loved one's handicap.

Just in time to use parts of it, with her permission, this letter came from a creative, happy young woman in Missouri:

Dear Genie Price,

I am a twenty-five-year-old who's a victim of cerebral palsy and confined to a wheelchair most of the time, except for walks I sometimes take using an A crutch inside our house. But please don't feel sorry for me! I think I must surely be one of the luckiest people God ever made! My wonderful mom and I live alone. My dad passed away as the result of a heart attack in 1957.

I've just been having a marvellous time with your book *The Wider Place*. This is not a letter about my handicap. It is a letter about my freedom. . . .

This young lady had grasped the message of freedom while sitting in her wheelchair. She had typed page after page—each filled with her joyous comments on certain chapters, although typing is obviously real work for her. My heart soared, and all I could think as I read was that here is a *free*, intelligent spirit—a happy child of God. And I must add that she probably could not be this way if her mother, who carries her responsibility alone now, were not a happy, intelligent, free spirit too.

Her comments on one or two chapters of the book are self-explanatory:

At the beginning of Chapter 1, it says: *God grants liberty only to those who love it.* (Daniel Webster) *So, if the Son liberates you—makes you free men—you are really and unquestionably free!*

How true I have found this to be in my own life. I can sit in my wheelchair and feel so sorry for those people walking around who have never known, never experienced the real freedom Christ gives, would give to them, if they would only trust Him and ask in simple, childlike *faith*.

Concerning the gist of another chapter, she wrote:

You said, Genie, that *God is not the author of confusion; He is, in Jesus Christ, the light of the world; the clarification of man's perplexities. This is the liberating news.* I certainly know that God is not the author of confusion! I have had cerebral palsy since birth, so I at least know what He has taught *me* through it. I know I am not confused because otherwise I might have been so much slower to learn about the true liberty I now enjoy. . . . I am a living example of the unchanging truth that God wants to go all the way with us in making us free. Some people don't believe it, but I now have a real and lasting purpose for my life.

You also wrote in *The Wider Place: Why do we go on expecting the worst? According to Jesus Christ, there need only be the joy of expecting the best—not according to what we imagine we want, but according to what God knows to be the best.* To that, I can only add that Jesus knows how to make the best out of the worst life can hand us. Your new book is going to be right, Genie. At least, here is one child of God who doesn't need a "pat answer" for her affliction. I'm having too much fun learning to be free in the midst of it!

As I sit here rereading her letter, I find only the perplexing, blood-tingling, tumultuous joy which makes no sense at all to those who keep trying to cause God to "make sense" with us. Thinking of this young lady, words like activist, explorer, and adventurer pop into my mind. Words such as those about a twenty-five-year-old confined to a wheelchair Just as there is no pat answer to her affliction, so there is none for her joy—none that can be curbed by words.

On a recent trip to Atlanta, I learned of the suicide of a young man in his early thirties. As a small boy he had been paralyzed from his waist down by polio. He lived with his affliction as long as he could and then took steps to end it. His sister told me that since the Salk vaccine had made the crippling disease of polio almost unheard of now, her brother's bitterness had increased until he took his life. He wanted an explanation of *why* the crippler of little children had not been controlled in time to prevent his tragedy.

I understood his desperation.

I also thought of a dear friend whom I haven't seen now for many years—Roger Winter, the author of *I'll Walk Tomorrow*. I met Rog and his lovely wife, Tres, not long after this once strapping athlete had been stricken with polio, so that for the remainder of his life he will be able to move only his head. Every so often Tres slips a contraption around Rog's neck to help his breathing. In order to speak, he has to "pump himself" up a little until that span of breath is "talked out", then pump again. He types with a specially curved stick in his mouth and handles his own business from home. And now he has written his story. I've lost count of the copies I've bought, I know the story well, but each time

I give away my last copy, I have to order more because I go on learning so much from what Roger Winter has learned in the years since we've been friends. You see, I know how bitter he was at first—how bitter and frightened, lying helplessly in that iron lung. I know the questions that tortured his mind.

I also know some of the questions other people used to ask me about this young man. "If he's such a terrific Christian, why doesn't God heal him?" "Roger Winter is a member of a church which believes in physical healing? How come he hasn't been healed?"

In his book, *I'll Walk Tomorrow*, Rog writes of a letter he once received from a correspondent whose own spiritual stability appeared shaken by the fact that Rog wasn't impatient at *not* being healed. This person wrote: "God can't use you until you are healed!"

"I have thought back to that statement many times," Roger says, "reflecting on all that has happened in my life since that day. It is obvious now that the author of the letter had underestimated God. When conditions are set by man, they limit the power of Christ within us. . . . What Jesus Christ has done in my life is to convert a potential tragedy into a meaningful, joyful event."

How could he write that last line? Is there a sensible answer as to how almost total paralysis for life can be converted "into a meaningful, joyful event"?

An answer, yes, but not a humanly sensible one.

Is it enough to say that had this disease not struck Roger Winter, his Christian witness would have been far less effective? Does God really think this way *before* a tragedy strikes? Does your intelligence permit you to believe that God is like this? Is He so limited that He has to sit on some remote throne and make decisions such as: "Now, let me see, I'll afflict Roger Winter with polio so that he will never be able to draw a breath again without conscious effort, and *then* he will be a fruitful witness for me"?

Roger was headed for football stardom. Wouldn't it have brought far more glory to God if, in answer to the prayers for divine healing which have ascended in Rog's behalf, God *had* healed him?

Or are we to resort to the ancient, masochistic, once widely held religious belief that only in his state of rigid *incapacity* could Roger Winter have been taught patience and self-denial?

Isn't God able to teach us anything He wants us to learn, no matter whether our lives are tragic or uneventful? In fact, most of us live rather uneventful lives. What about us? Doesn't God want us to be taught patience and courage too?

Do you see?

There are no answers the human intelligence can accept which cover the problem of the handicapped, either. No separate answers for this tragedy and that. No line of questioning and no line of reasoning which does not slam ultimately into a thick wall of silence.

Roger Winter believes healing *must* be sought. Typical of his fine, rational mind, he reminds us that there's no other way to obtain it. "But," he warns, "even the greatest amount of faith can only carry us to the point of God's touch. It is for Him to extend His healing power as it best suits our total life." Knowing Roger Winter, I'm sure he would agree with this addition: Only God knows what suits.

Handicapped persons, such as Roger and my new young friend with cerebral palsy, who are joyful, interested, and creative have simply come to the place of letting God decide. That explanation of mine may also seem a bit pat, and perhaps it is. But these two have stopped the bitter questioning. They have exchanged questioning for questing—and from wheelchairs, they are both romping in their minds and in their spirits—finding the exploration good and the treasures infinite.

Chapter 9

Doubt

There is no moral power in doubt and questioning, but both can lead somewhere if we do not become entrenched in them. Ruts wear quickly in our brains, and the habit of doubt and questioning can land us *in* those ruts unless we see to it that we stay in motion.

The use of the word questioning must be clarified. I do not mean *questing* or *searching*, but rather the type of question hurling that is motivated by pain, sorrow, disappointment, disillusionment, or bitterness within us. The kind of questioning which invariably leads to doubt because to that kind of question, hurled in bitterness or pain, there is no easy answer—often no answer at all. But, as we will attempt to develop in the final chapter, such questioning—any questioning—can end or be dampened down so that we can live with it in a kind of wordless new involvement with what we can understand of the nature of God.

I am convinced that the average, normal-minded human being (as "normal-minded" as any of us know ourselves to be) can discover and make the leap over into this new involvement with the altogether loving Power behind our universe. If this suddenly sounds farfetched, too philosophical—wait. If this Power, in your present shattered circumstances, does not appear to be loving, this does not change the fact that He is. So, wait;

think it through; lay all your own doubts out before you right now and be honest about them—not guilty because of them, merely honest. And, at least, hopeful. I am not writing only to those among you who doubt the existence of such a God, nor to those who only half believe. This is for everyone, including those of us who thankfully call ourselves Christians. Tragedy, disappointment, disillusionment, and anguish of any kind can turn anyone at anytime into at least a temporary doubter. It's ridiculous to hide this, but too many Christians try to make it appear that the idea of doubt never crosses their minds. That's unreal, and ultimately only the pretender is hurt by such a practice, although those around him can be injured too—disillusioned—when at that crash in the "non-doubters" life, he crumples. This type of glib non-doubter repels the seeker too. Unreality repels; reality draws. If we believe we are doubt*less*, we are simply self-deceived. "Lord, I believe; help thou mine unbelief" is one of the sanest, most truthful prayers ever spoken.

Only continuing doubt damages. Honest doubt can be, with God involved, the path to certainty. Thomas, once he was truly convinced, remained unshakeable. The fact that Jesus had to make a special appearance for Thomas' sake was not too much effort for the Saviour. No effort towards us is ever "too much" for Him. Thomas wasn't being a spoiled, stubborn brat or an arrogant agnostic. He held honest doubts, which, once dispelled, set him free to believe. God will do this for anyone.

Here we should recognize that God-doubt, flabby faith, and spiritual uncertainty aren't the only kinds of doubt we're considering. *Self-doubt* can be one of the most destructive, painful experiences in any life. Yet often, self-doubt is inevitable for a time. I've experienced it, and so have you. Some of us are too insecure to admit self-doubt, which state, of course, leads to boasting. But I am referring to the kind of honest self-doubt which comes as a result of a sickening failure, of having lost one's position suddenly—either at work or socially. One of the most painful kinds of self-doubt haunts the sleepless nights of the divorcee whose husband, after years of marriage to her, suddenly finds someone else who "understands him". Parents agonize in self-doubt when their children are arrested or when their daughters become pregnant before marriage.

I have to struggle through my own periods of self-doubt when the public passes up a new book of mine like a fast freight going west. When the Inland Revenue indulges in one of its favourite pastimes, examining and re-examining a single woman whose annual income varies widely according to how fast that public passes her new book or how many of them take it home, I foolishly, and without any valid reason, get so frightened that I begin to doubt myself! Even though I know I have not tried to fudge one penny's worth in reporting my income, it still frightens me.

Broken love affairs, divorces, financial inadequacies, lost jobs—failures of any kind rightly or wrongly cause self-doubt. So, welcome to the human race!

Doubt harboured where other people are concerned usually leads to cynicism, a horrible disease of the mind. My own tendency has been to trust people too much—stupidly, unthinkingly. This is dangerous too, believe me, and eventually can lead to another form of self-doubt.

Should we doubt other people until they've proven themselves to us? No. But we should consider and act upon the fact that if anyone, anywhere on the earth had been totally trustworthy in God's sight, Jesus wouldn't have needed to die. To recognize and act upon the fact of human frailty is only sane. It's really true, you know, that no one is perfect. One big, crushing disillusionment can twist an entire life out of shape, can turn a trusting person into a doubting cynic. "I loved her more than any human being on earth," a woman once told me, "until I found out that she discussed my problem of alcoholism at her prayer group! I despise her now and all her religious, praying kind."

I understand that, but it's foolish. People who get together to pray *can* be damaging ladies and gentlemen. Normally they are not, but they can be. They're human too, and "in order to pray more intelligently" they tell tales and mention names as though the Lord didn't know already.

Continuing doubt, for any reason, can destroy us. Anyone who tries to live on it will die, both morally and spiritually—and, I dare to say, intellectually. Doubt is negative. It has no life and no motion, except backwards. We can miss most of life's fulfilment if we hang back and refuse to try a thing because we doubt our ability to do it. Cynicism, chronic doubt of other people, can rob us of ever finding love, friendship, or peace.

Has it ever occurred to you that most doubting people are vain, arrogant, demanding—even in their personalities? Oh, they may speak softly, hang back, appear shy, reticent, even scared, but bascially they are vain. Why? Because in order to dispense with *their* doubts, God and their fellow-man have to come up with a lot more proof of *their* worth than has yet been offered to the human race as a whole.

The truly great souls are not doubters. They are not doubters of God, themselves, or their fellow-man. They are more like children—more like Jesus said we all had to become before we could enter the kingdom of God—the kingdom of love, peace, and inner quiet. "Except ye . . . become as little children, ye shall not enter into the kingdom of heaven," He said. What did He really mean by that? Did Jesus mean that we were to become guileless? I don't think so, since He, of all people, knew that no mere human being could *become* guileless—could suddenly switch himself around so as to have no more tricky thoughts, no inclination to white lies, no smallness in his nature. Did Jesus mean that we were to become dependent, as little children are dependent? Yes, in part. But do you really think we can *will* dependence? It's an established fact that children are born dependent. So, how could we change ourselves from the state of *interdependence* (the desired state of an adult) back to the total dependence of a child?

Then, what did Jesus mean?

At this point in my own pilgrimage, I believe He meant that we are somehow to become *trusting*. Until a parent disillusions a child by promising something he doesn't deliver or is caught by that child in a lie of convenience or otherwise, the child *trusts* his father or his mother and expects care and love. Trust, the ability, the capacity for believing, seems to be inherent. Only when some event occurs to shake that capacity for trust is it weakened. If a first experience of disillusionment is major and strikes deeply into the child's mind, the pattern for doubt can begin. But my interpretation of what

Jesus said leads me to believe that on the whole we are *born to believe*.

A look at the achievers of the world—not necessarily financial achievers—the men and women who have, by their creative lives, their intellects, their skills, added to life for the rest of us, will show that they were mainly persons of childlike minds. Not accepting everything as a matter of course without a tendency to healthy doubt (inquiry), but with minds humble before the truth, uncluttered, never self-protective, open, able to learn. Someone once said, "It is Newton who sees himself as a child on the seashore and his discoveries in the coloured shells." An irrevocable kind of delight follows such openness. A child's delight, unpinched by doubt or vanity, free to know joy, to continue "on the seashore" all the way to the end.

Contributors to our world whom we call great, such as Newton, shared the trait of *being able to believe in something*. After all, unless we can believe in an *absolute*, we can never add to our knowledge. There must be a point of beginning—something to which we can fasten—a polestar, a place to centre down. If you do not believe that $1 + 1 = 2$, then how can you learn that $2 + 2 = 4$? You can't.

There must be a foundation on which to build before the building begins; a point of departure before any journey; a launching pad, to our space-oriented minds. A collection of unrelated facts, superstitions, and clichés won't do. That's a junk pile. A solid launching pad is as essential to a flight to the moon as the space craft itself. So, we must have a solid basis on which to begin the journey through our years. A happy, trustworthy family life can start a child on its way quite safely, but never with entire safety, because there is no such human phenomenon as a perfectly loving, trustworthy parent. Thus, the universal flaw in believing takes over: *doubt*. The capacity for doubt seems inherent too, and at an early age we learn how to use this doubt-capacity simply by being in the midst of the human race. As we have said, the ability to doubt must be stirred up from outside, but we develop it quickly as one of our first acts of self-protection. If we can fall back on doubt, less is expected of us—or so we think. "She lied to me once. Boy, I'm not going to try *that* again!"

So, perhaps what Jesus meant was that unless and until we somehow return to the open-hearted, first dawn of childhood where *to trust* is natural, we cannot go on to what He has in store for us.

Is it really true that much of what we can call *spiritual doubt* is due to stubbornness on our part? To sin? To a blanket refusal to believe God for fear of what *we* might have to do about it?

I tried using a smoke screen of doubt once in my own life and for this very reason. In one certain area, I had decided to take the reins back in my hands and out of God's. I persuaded myself that I was doing the "best thing under the circumstances", but I also was so convinced that I was wrong, that I heard myself railing out at a friend: "God hasn't touched my life *at all*, so why shouldn't I go on with my rein jerking?" I suppose my need of a Saviour had been great enough and *conscious* enough that I didn't get by with this long enough to do any permanent damage. I kept on with my railing for quite awhile though. Then I cried from anger and frustration. Then I laughed. If my friend had taken me seriously and had launched into much counselling, text-flinging, and prayer for "the real thing" to happen to me—as though it hadn't—I might have dug some deep doubt-ruts in my own brain. Doubting might have become a crutch, a gimmick to get my own way. Before long, I might really have doubted that I *had* encountered the living Christ.

But I had begun my life with Jesus simply. There were no proof texts and no indoctrination and no institutional recognition of the encounter. I wasn't in a church, and I "went forward" *only* towards Him because it suddenly dawned on me that He was coming towards me. Nothing was said about "the plan of salvation" or faith healing or baptism by sprinkling, pouring, or immersion, and I had no words with which to witness, except that "I've met Him! I've met Him!" Before that moment, I had argued glibly that Christians couldn't possibly be right; that the resurrected Jesus story from Sunday school days insulted my intelligence.

Then there was this resurrected Jesus *coming towards me*.

For me, real doubt of the fact of Christ and His involvement with my life has not come often. I find doubt extremely hard, and hard *on* me. Mainly, I find it difficult to doubt Jesus Christ because my initial involvement with Him was *personal*.

This is the age of experiential expression of life. Our young people demand to experience what they are asked to accept. So, even though some theologians may not agree, I can only share what I know. Having written six books based on the Scriptures, I am convinced experiential expression is authentic. I met Jesus Christ with no academic knowledge of what was happening to me. This is only one way to become a believer, and perhaps not the best way, but it is the way by which I came. It is what I know, and so I write of it when the circumstances are apt—as here. Doubt of Christ's life and His place in my life has been no problem to me. For one thing, I have a believing nature; for another, the encounter with Him was real.

Oh, I've had frightening doubts, especially during the first years after my conversion, as to whether I would "make it" or not. But this had nothing to do with doubting God. I just didn't know Him well enough yet to know whether it was His voice saying, "Turn to the right" or "Turn to the left", or the voice of some well-meaning Christian who had decided beforehand how my fruits should hang on my new "spiritual" tree. We do great harm to new Christians by "getting their guidance" for them. We inadvertently foster a kind of spiritual pride in them by inferring or declaring that the outward changes have to come either before or along with the inner changes. I was proud of breaking certain habits at once, and then torn with self-doubt when the temptations *or* habits returned. If only we could learn to leave new Christians to God! Only He knows what certain attachments mean to them. Only He knew what the rich young ruler had to give up—and when.

"Why does my religious wife keep yakking at me for having a couple of glasses of beer before I go to bed at night? Sure, I know I'm too fat, but so is she! I don't say a word when she bakes a lemon pie and sits down to eat the whole thing herself. Where does she get the idea that beer makes you fatter than pie?"

I suppose I will battle the weight problem for the rest of my life, too. But I certainly feel I have no right to "tell" anyone else that God approves or disapproves of one bad habit or another as long as I carry even *ten pounds* of excess weight. By playing God with other people, we can create the *growing conditions* for real or imagined doubt.

A mother wrote the following lines to a friend of mine. "We've had prayer for the healing of my son's eyes over and over, but he's still blind. Why did Jesus heal when He was on earth and then refuse to do it now? I'm losing my faith, that's what. *My doubts* are terrible."

And here is a quotation from an Associated Press story headlined: SHE REGAINS SIGHT IN SUDDEN "MIRACLE". " 'No one quite knows how it happened,' says Barbara Bubar, mother of two, telling how she regained her sight after growing progressively blind since childhood. 'My husband and I went to a movie,' the 35-year-old woman said. 'Suddenly I started to see lights. I walked outside and I read a sign in a window across the street. I gulped a few times—at supper I couldn't even see the table or my family around it. A few hours later I'm reading signs and number plates.' "

The article goes on to say that this woman had undergone a cornea transplant, but scar tissue had formed behind the transplant, blocking all vision. Then—what this woman called her "miracle". She was seeing her children clearly for the first time. Her doctors had no explanation, but Barbara Bubar said, "God did it. He answered my prayers."

Did He? Was this a miracle to stimulate faith in this woman? Doesn't God care about the blind eyes of the other woman's little boy? Of course, He does. You know by now that I have focused on this seeming contradiction in God's love for a reason: *There are no pat answers*.

I'm always glad when anyone gives God the credit, when anyone shows renewed faith, for whatever reason, but is this what real faith is all about? Didn't St. Paul say we were to give thanks in *everything*? The good and the bad? The joyous and the disappointing? In gain and loss?

Dare we depend upon "miracles" to dispel our doubts? Now, we have no reason to think that the woman who joyously recovered her sight had doubts, even though she had lost all her vision. Perhaps her faith was still strong. Who knows? But is this the ultimate test of faith?

Isn't the main issue—God Himself? And don't we ignore Him when we search wildly for specific answers to our specific sorrows?

Is all doubt bad? Doubt has been called the shadow of truth. Could there be two kinds of doubt: honest doubt, which may well be the shadow of truth, and dishonest doubt, such as the kind I once used as a cover-up?

I hope you'll think this through. I'm going to—for a long, long time, before approaching the final chapter.

Chapter 10

The One Answer

Some of the problems in our lives do not get solved. They keep returning, and our hearts break again and again. The pain does not lessen with the repetition, but we do learn from it. I have two dear friends who are facing just such a recurring heartbreak, and each time they emerge with more courage. The sorrow carves out room for more faith and confidence in God's minute by minute involvement.

Often, because I love these people, I have wanted desperately to come up with an answer for them—an explanation—a theory which would bring instant peace. But there is none, and I have refused the temptation because I am sick of glib responses and sense the danger of spreading the darkness in a pat answer flipped out when trouble strikes—the pat retorts of the "answer flingers".

I began my Christian life being just such an "answer flinger" because I heard other people doing it—other Christians whose lives I respected. My own encounter with Jesus Christ had so changed life for me that for a long time I thought I was *supposed* to be able to convince everyone who came to talk that they could and would be changed too if only they would do so and so and such and such. Because I had written two or three books, many people were suddenly asking me questions, and I felt somehow I would be failing God if I didn't dig for some kind of quick answer. Most of my compulsion, of course, was due to immaturity, but it seems strange to me now, with the perspective of the years, that *speed* was also a part of it. My speaking schedule was too crowded; I rushed from airport to railroad station. There wasn't much time—certainly no time to *think*. Just hurry up and find something to say, or find a strong last line for your letter to that worried woman so she'd feel instant relief. I did want with all my heart to provide an answer, so I tried.

It's good to be almost free of this—to have been getting freer of it for more than a decade—because now I know I am on safe ground *only* when I direct attention to Jesus Christ Himself.

I am on safe ground only when I direct attention to Jesus Christ Himself.

I repeated that sentence for a reason: the reason for writing this book in the first place—a one-tracked book which says only one thing: Beware of trying to operate on a pat answer, even if it is couched in the so-called "liberated" language of today, making it appear new.

I do feel God's people are becoming more and more enlightened and open to fresh ideas, and I'm in favour of any approach that will stir up the mind to think in the presence of the Eternal God. But just because an unusual presentation of some truth about God makes it *sound* new doesn't mean that its content is new, for truth about God is as old as God, and He *is* the beginning. We don't need *new truth*; we need to begin to act on what Jesus Christ *has always been*.

We don't need to employ contemporary jargon in order to bring enlightenment. Enlightenment came when Jesus came! Enlightenment is here now in His Spirit—more real than the sunlight flooding my yard and breaking into the woods around my house. "I am come a light into the world, that whosoever believeth on me should not abide in darkness." We don't need *new light*; we need to begin to act on the fact of the Light already with us, around us, and in us in the presence of Jesus Christ.

When tragedy strikes us, this great Light swings back and forth illuminating the *One Answer*: our desperate need for a new kind of involvement with Jesus Christ, who has always *been* truth.

No matter how long you've known Him, there is still more ahead for you. No matter how long I've known Him, there is more for me. More and more and more. And when do we need that *more* as we need it in the hour of trouble, of heartache, of despair? This ever-freshening involvement seems best described as a kind of *wordless* involvement—an inner-knowing. An inner kind of person-to-person "being together" where you and I can weep, cry out, struggle, even rebel—*with Christ.*

I mean it when I contend that if it helps you to believe that God *sent* your tragedy in order to *perfect you*, "burn out your dross", cling to that. But will you be open enough to consider for a moment that there might be *more* than the action of God lighting a fire, you suffering in the flames, and you emerging pure gold? Isn't it more creative, more like the Creator Himself, to help us shift the emphasis away from ourselves—to *him*?

Let me try to explain. Jesus Christ came and lived

among us and suffered and died for more reasons than we will ever be able to comprehend as long as we are earthbound. But He *did* come as a *Redeemer*, so isn't it more like Him to act in a redemptive way in our times of heartbreak? Did Job say, "I know that my *disciplinarian* liveth?"

God wants us free of our imperfections; He wants this more than we want it. But if He suffered for us, is it like Him to force us to repeat what He already endured in order to make us more like Him? If it is true that "by His stripes we are healed", do you really believe Christ sends human suffering *only* to "perfect us"? Were His hours on the cross not enough? How much more like Him it is for God to act lovingly, tenderly, redemptively in the midst of our suffering—taking the blow for us.

I repeat, if it is of more comfort to you to believe that He sent your heartache in order to purify you, keep that comfort. I write here for those of us who don't get enought solace from that. I submit this for those of us who might be quieted, in some measure at least, by the shifted emphasis, by looking at it this way: The accident occurred; the loved one is gone. The telephone rang; the cherished dream is broken. Jesus knows it all—knew before we knew. He is here, waiting to *be* the Redeemer in this too. Not to make us feel fine in a few minutes; not to put the dream back together or negate the accident—but *to begin the moment we are ready to make creative, redemptive use of what has happened*. To begin, just as soon as we are able and willing, to give us ways in which to *use* the sorrow so that not one groan or tear will be wasted.

If I am thus involved *with Him* in the redemptive process, I do not have time to demand an answer as to why the dream smashed; why the accident occurred; why that loved one fell ill; why the aged person is not set free. You see, there is a great difference between being peaceful and being passive. And the God of love is never passive; He is always on the move. He never wastes a moment brooding over either. His troubles with us or our troubles with life or ourselves. He is always in motion because He *is* love, and just as soon as we are willing, He wants to set us in motion *in love* towards someone else in need.

"I sometimes feel I can't bear the sight of those familiar hospital corridors after the weeks I spent there when my husband was dying of cancer," a friend said last year. "But I'm going! I don't feel able to go. All I really want to do is stay home and cry, but I'm going to be a Grey Lady. I'm sure God has told me to get up and go, whether I feel ready or not."

She went, and this woman has had an extra touch of redemptive love for other women walking those same corridors because she has been where they are now. God gave her the strength to be in the minute she was willing, and together they have been in motion in love ever since.

This love activity can begin during the first hours of grief or any kind of human despair. Even when we are resting on our beds (or trying to) from the peculiarly painful exhaustion which accompanies despair, Jesus begins the activity *towards* us—in love. He is always ready, and gradually we will be able to realize His healing movement towards us, *if we've glimpsed Him as He really is*.

There is no real two-way involvement in any relationship without motion, but for our part, the only activity necessary when the blow first falls is that inner-turning to Him for help. No *words* need pass between God and us in this kind of involvement. I deal in words, and yet I have lived through times when none were possible. None. Do we always have to be saying something? Do we talk too much—even to God? I think so. Do we expect too much "talk" from Him? Yes. His promise was that He would be *with us*: "Lo, I am with you always. . . ." Not, "Lo, I will be always talking to you, comforting you, perfecting you, explaining to you."

I will be with you.

He will answer our needs, but not necessarily with words. This wordless, silent, active kind of involvement with the One who created us does change things—in you—in me.

Perhaps we don't even notice the changes, and this is good. There is always the danger of over-subjectivity with the other emphasis: that God sent the heartache in order to perfect us. *He is always busy about the task of perfecting us* as we plod through our difficult times. I have grown in mine, and I'm sure you have. But I, for one, would probably grow far less quickly if my attention focused on: "What is He going to do to 'perfect' *me*?" I've found that He does His best work in us when we're too occupied with *loving* to notice ourselves one way or another.

It seems to me that Jesus was deliberately making this shift in emphasis in His remark after healing the young man "blind from his birth". You remember, the disciples had asked him: "Master, who did sin, this man or his parents, that he was born blind?" (These *were* Jesus' disciples, don't forget—with *their* emphasis in the unanswerable place too!) Jesus' reply is memorable and loaded with meaning: "Neither hath this man sinned, nor his parents: but that the works of God should be made manifest in him."

Surely, Jesus, who knew that "all have sinned and come short of the glory of God", did not mean that these parents and their son were sinless creatures. He seemed to be attempting to shock His own disciples into putting their question another way—or forgetting it altogether. To me, Jesus was saying, in effect: "No one's sin has anything to do with what happened to this boy's sight or with what I'm about to do. He is simply blind, and I am going to heal him, and then you can all see with your own eyes that God is working."

He is simply blind. The accident simply happened. The dream simply crashed. But Jesus is there—ready to reveal what God can do—in the midst of it. To me, the whole concept of God punishing through human affliction was knocked flat by that one statement which shifted the emphasis entirely.

On the semi-tropical island where I live, in summer the woods become choked with a great variety of undergrowth—weeds, seedling trees, and vines. When winter comes, the lush, tangled undergrowth begins to die back. It is as though Nature "clears the woods". In my own small patch of undeveloped land, I can see great oaks and hickories standing out in full light after their long warm months in the shadowy "glooms". All summer I rather miss this view of the big trees, and then they are there for me again: towering landmarks in the winter sun which is free to pour its beams all the way down on to the forest floor so that the roots of the wildflowers and the grapevines will be warmed, readied for spring. I like the freed light streaming into the shadows. I respond to the sight of the huge, certain trees again. Odd perhaps, but for all the years I've lived here, this "clearing" of the undergrowth quiets me inside —makes me feel ready.

Writing this book has had a similar effect. No matter how familiar my own agonized questions have become, no matter how much steam they have enabled me to blow off in the past by shouting, or at least thinking: "Why did this have to happen to me?"—I am now more prepared to stop the crying. A little frightened and somewhat missing my "undergrowth", but winter comes for us all at certain periods in our lives, and it's better then, when the winds scream and the rains rush down, for some light to get through. Far better, when the storms come, to be able to see the big trees standing.

If you have attempted to read this while passing through a crisis, perhaps the big trees aren't visible to you yet. That's all right. Put the book away until you can think more clearly. But don't put it away until you have read it through. Even if it doesn't reach you now, please read it.

The big trees are there for you, too, just as they are there for me. Give yourself time to break the Why? habit. I have managed, by Grace, through four bad times without the word even rising in my heart. Habits can be broken, but they must be replaced with better ones—in this instance, the habit of *realizing* the potential of the inwards turning to God instead of demanding an answer to our Whys.

If you are still filled with doubts, don't add to your burden by worrying about it. I've thought a long time between the writing of the preceding chapter and this one, and during that time one of my dearest and most valued friends, Anna B. Mow, called long distance. Once more, through my beloved Anna, God gave me just what I needed when I needed it. I was thinking about *doubt*. Anna began to talk to me about it, and I took notes.

"Honest doubt," she said, "is when you take what you believe or have always been taught to believe and compare it with ideas you've never thought about before—other people's opinions or concepts which so far had escaped you. You re-examine your own way and then *compare*. Some of what you have always believed or thought you believed creates doubt in your mind. This is *honest doubt*. It sets you *wondering*, and this hurts no one! In the long run, you may keep all your old concepts, but then you may not. You may add to them from the new, but you are growing as you wonder and think about the new idea. Once you've reached your conclusion—decided what you really believe—it then belongs to you in a way the old *taught* beliefs did not. This is honest doubt, and it is not bad."

You are growing as you wonder and think about the new idea.

I hope what has been written here so far has created some honest doubt in you—doubt concerning the wisdom of being too quick to decide you need or even want a pat answer. It is *not* a sin to question, although it may be sinful to answer in a way which will not stand the test of either time or reality.

We must realize that even honest, healthy doubt which can ultimately move us towards new freedom and confidence in God may temporarily cause a sense of despair. Especially if our old, familiar answers have become such a part of us that we're afraid to let them go. The temporary despair during the uneasy period need not last; indeed, it won't last, and yet many Christians have often been made to feel guilt over what is a normal process.

Right here we face squarely the need to recognize the difference between demanding a *reason* why a crisis occurred and faith in what may be God's *purpose* in it. We dwell on the *Why*; God dwells on the *What*. We cry out to know the reason why this dreadful affliction came our way. God answers: I am working in your affliction. I have a purpose: ". . . that the works of God should be made manifest." This difference between "the reason *for*" and "God's purpose *in*" must be delineated.

If we have made this delineation, *if* we have established once and for all that honest questioning, honest doubting are not sin—are, in fact, normal in times of stress—*if* we have it straight that *there are no quick, valid, patterned answers*, we are ready to begin the discovery of the One Real Answer.

I do not mean to imply that it is likely any one of us will "advance" to the place where we never long for nor feel the need to give or receive a pat answer. In all of us there is an innate desire for an answer to our Whys. There *is* the One Answer, but we shout for *specifics*. By the same token, there is a deeply embedded desire to *give* a satisfactory, seemingly logical answer. Think back to the heartbroken mother whose child died of leukaemia. I'm positive the bumbling Christian who assured her that God "took" her baby because He is a jealous God *meant* to be "helping"; he or she felt some sort of inner need to help.

I recall telling my friend, Frances Pitts, in a letter I wrote when her aged mother died that she should give thanks for all the years she did have with her. I wasn't wrong, for this is what Frances is doing *now*. But she is only able to do it two years later! What I wrote wasn't wrong; my timing was wrong. What I said must have been only an irritant *then*. Her mother had just died, and Frances hadn't had time for recovery of any kind. She knew the One Answer, and He was right there with her, waiting until she was *able* to get her attention back on Him—even if only for a few minutes at a time. Christ is always wiser than we. He didn't try to remind her, as I did, of something her mind could not assimilate. He waited.

I felt the need *within me* to say something to help my friend, to ease her pain. Was this wrong? Of course not. God puts these longings in our hearts. But it is wrong to try too hard to think up something *specific* which may only harm. I'm sure now that I should have said something like: "You know I'm with you as much as I can be, with all the miles between us, because I care about you. Most important, I know you know Jesus is there . . . right there."

Instead, I jumped at "words of comfort" without checking first with Him. I trusted myself to know what to say.

Time does not heal; *time dims*. But God *uses* our time trap in the healing process. He knows how to wait, while our tendency is to say something fast—anything at all, just so it's something. Am I inferring that ministers, priests, and others in the religious life should never offer words of comfort? That's a ridiculous question, but I thought I'd ask it anyway. Words of comfort can and do help. The point here is that many of us don't hesitate to fling out the same words time after time, with no thought of what God might be trying to *tell* us to say.

After all, *Jesus Christ is in this thing with us*. He will prompt us, but He has to get our attention first.

Have you heard someone say: "She was just too good to live on this old earth. God must have needed her in heaven."

Sounds comforting, but think: Why would God take goodness from the earth?

"I'm sorry. Oh, I'm sorry," might give a lot more comfort—for *that* moment. "I'm here. I'm here with you," may help even more. It is not an answer of any kind. It is a statement of welcome fact; it is quiet; it is reassuring; and it is true.

I seriously doubt that any of us can ever learn this kind of direct simplicity until we begin to concentrate more and more upon the One Answer Himself: Jesus Christ. We do not learn *faith*. *He creates it in us*. ". . . the author and finisher of our faith" *is* Jesus Christ, and He ". . . is not the author of confusion."

The answer, the One Answer, when tragedy strikes, when sorrow overshadows even our inner light, is *faith*—confidence in Jesus Christ—a quiet confidence just knowing that He is there. That's why this book was written. We have come to expect the poetic, complex, profound "word of comfort"—the intellectually acceptable philosophy of an answer *on our own terms*. There is no such answer.

The One Answer is *confidence* in the living God.

Confidence grows slowly, if it is real. I suppose this is why we go on demanding an instant cure for all human hardship. We have cultivated the art of waiting with *confidence*. We're in a hurry to stop suffering.

And why not? No one in his right mind enjoys suffering. When pain comes, we want to hurry it away, to rush some kind of happiness and peace into its place. I recall what my friend, Frances, said about her recent discovery which is bringing, at last, some release from grief: "I kept trying to be happy again, the way it was when my mom was still here. I was pushing for even a small hope that there might be another phase of my life when I'd be happy and carefree once more." At this point, I interrupted and handed her part of this chapter to read. "You're dead right," she said, her eyes snapping. "I was pushing for instant, familiar happiness again! It isn't realistic to do that. Jesus may not live in time, but He sure knows we do! Jesus knew that only now would I be able even to begin to accept *acceptance*."

See any signs of either a pat answer or a futile questioning here? And yet my friend's initial questions were the usual ones. During the first months of her grieving, I received letter after letter in which she wondered if she'd ever know the presence of Christ again; that she wasn't at all sure about life after death, etcetera. He understood that, too, and He waited until He knew she could think again. She had no sense of His presence, but He had a sense of hers because He was there—not weary of the waiting.

Slowly, steadily, stubbornly this woman is working and living her way back into an even stronger *confidence* in the living God than before her sorrow came. She's been inching along for more than two years, but there is movement all the way.

Just as there is movement—joyous, adventuresome movement—in the life of my new young friend as she sits hour after hour, day after day in her wheelchair. There are no answers to human suffering, but there *is*—for anyone—the bright, freeing potential of a growing confidence in God.

There is another aspect of the meaning of the word *confidence*. We have faith in someone if we have *confidence* in that person, but we can also give ourselves *in confidence*—a moment or a lifetime of *confiding in*—and I mean far more than sharing a secret. When we share a *confidence*, something of us goes along. We do not, or we should not, share confidences with someone in whom we have no confidence. Anyone knows the danger of that. And here the word *confidence* becomes truly interchangeable with the word *faith*.

If we trust someone, sharing ourselves with him or with her is no struggle; it's the most natural thing to do.

Then why is faith in God so hard for us when our lives fall apart?

Is it because we feel that He, being God, should have done better by us? Or could it be because we didn't know Him well enough before the tragedy struck? Were never entirely sure about His intentions towards us? Had never "seen Him plain"? Do we find faith difficult because God has been distorted into a remote, nearly inaccessible Force too hard to convince, too far away to reach when we're suddenly so tired, so filled with sorrow and despair? Have the twisted, man-concocted concepts of God's "will" put God out of reach without our knowing it was happening? Have regular church attendance and the repetition of the same hymns and creeds become so automatic and dullness has set in—dullness too tough to cut through when our energy is in such short supply?

Do we, perhaps way in the back of our mind, still cling to the ancient distortion that God punishes by affliction?

Have we eaten so much cake and drunk so much coffee in the church "fellowship halls" that we've forgotten the Man of Galilee who was often hungry and had no place to lay His head?

Have we heard so much bickering about how to raise money that when we think of church we think of committees and budgets instead of poured-out blood and love?

Have we forgotten—or have we never known or believed—that a *real Person* once said—is still saying: "Come unto me, and I will give you rest ... *follow me.*"

Do we feel shut away from "the God of all comfort" because we really have never considered ourselves lost sheep in need of the Shepherd? If this new grief, this sudden affliction, this crushing disappointment or disillusionment causes us to admit our lostness for the first time, we can rejoice! Only the *lost* sheep cries for help. The Shepherd never forces His love upon anyone. He is always there loving, offering His grace, but He waits for us to turn around, out of curiosity or helpnessess, to find the source of all that love and grace.

I have heard about and have experienced those times, once the initial turning had been made, when God just works on to free us even without *any* conscious act on our part. "I am understanding," He said of Himself.

Far more clearly than we could ever understand our-selves, He understands our being too stricken even to turn to Him by a conscious word. Still, if we are His, and if through the days and years of our lives we have entered into the *wordless involvement*, the intimacy of real friendship with God, He will *draw* us when we are too helpless to pray—too blanketed by despair to remember one line of Scripture. The glorious habit of His friend-ship can become a part of us, so that when we find it impossible to concentrate, He will remind us of *His* unrelenting concentration on us—in love.

We are all so different that no two experiences of Christ in sorrow could be the same. Still, He is the same—exactly the same as He was yesterday before the sorrow came. Yesterday, today, and forever—this is the *absolute* on which we can depend. This is our point of departure on the new, strange journey through pain of any kind.

Perhaps someone is reading this page who has never experienced any closeness to the living God. If you have never been sure of the unalterable constancy of Jesus Christ, how can you know it in the midst of hard-ship—when you must need to know?

Anyone can enter at any time—even now—into the dynamic, intimate peace of the friendship with Jesus Christ. Words may help *you*, but they aren't essential as far as He's concerned. One wordless heart-cry directed to Him, and the friendship is begun. You won't need to shout or plead or cajole. Just ask in your heart, and His forgiveness will come because He is there at the scene of your suffering. You may or may not *feel* this forgiveness and peace, especially if your heart is broken, your emotions torn. But the strangeness is all on your side.

God has known you and loved you from the beginning. Any friendship takes a while to deepen, but He has been moving towards you in love for all the days of your life.

I hope many will read this book who are not in the midst of some sudden, shattering trial. You are not immune, though. No more immune than I to possible suffering ahead. It seems only sensible to begin to ready yourself, to learn how to be familiar with God now, before the trouble strikes.

In trouble or out of trouble, in sorrow or in pure joy, the human heart was created for this divine friendship. The "you" no one else really knows or understands; the eternal "you"; the part of you which will never die. Your *spirit*, perhaps, although I don't seem to need a label. The *self* of you which somehow, even in agony, struggles to go on to be free.

There are no patterned answers to your heart cries, but there is an all-inclusive answer to that one cry of "you" to be heard, to be listened to, to be understood, to be loved.

Jesus promised to be with us always, even to the end. . . .

Is this an answer?

It is the One Answer. He Himself is the answer, but unless you have made the connection from your side by faith, by confidence in His love, He waits—to forgive you, to quiet you, to gentle you, to give you peace again. Identity. Life. Life which will be merely interrupted when you leave this earth. A joyful interruption—swift, like the batting of an eye. Then—all of everything forever in His presence.

Don't berate yourself if you have no faith. Faith is not

a commodity which can be fought for or concocted. Faith, as I see it, is the unavoidable result of *knowing* God in Jesus Christ. Anyone who lives consciously in this friendship with Him soon stops thinking about the size of his or her faith. Jesus said this was irrelevant anyway. A mustard seed is pretty small. What matters is that our faith is in Him.

Faith begins with God's touch on us. He *is* the author of faith, and what He finishes will one day be perfect.

If you are choking on questions, ask your questions of Him. He is the One Answer. He will answer by giving you Himself.

The God of the outstretched arms does not condemn us for our human reactions to trouble. But those questions and those needs can be answered only *in Him*. I did not say *by Him*—in Him. Jesus did not even hint that He would write out the specific answers for us; mainly, I suppose, because He knew and knows that we usually ask the wrong questions. Our tendency is to become preoccupied with side issues. What He did promise is that in it all, He would be with us. *In* all of life with us, and, by His Spirit, *in* us, prompting us, giving us the will and the energy to follow Him.

Does it seem odd and unbelievable that the Son of God would want us close to Him every minute? He wants just that. Through both the tears and the joy of earth life, He is saying: "Follow me." He is saying, "Lo, I am with you always. . . ." At the end of this life, He will still want us with Him: "I go to prepare a place for you . . . that where I am, there ye may be also."

If Jesus Christ, God incarnate, wants to be with us that much, how can we resist?

Confidence in God does *not* mean we're going to feel

happy again in a few minutes. Jesus suffered on that cross. He even cried, "Why?" He knows deep human suffering, and He knows it does not end abruptly. Does it make any sense at all that *this* God would frown on or disapprove of our questions in the midst of our own suffering? The Father heard Jesus when He cried "Why?" The Father is still listening—still tending our confidence in Him as He tended His Son's that dark day at Calvary.

Jesus felt free to shout "Why?" at the Father because He *knew* His Father's heart, knew His every intention towards him—towards us all—forever and from the beginning. This knowing, this intimacy, this confidence which the Father understood left the Saviour free to question, but ultimately it *ended* His questioning. Knowing the depth and the height and the breadth of the love of God as He did, Jesus also felt free to commit His Spirit into the Father's hands—in total confidence—in faith.

"I am not Jesus Christ," you say. No. But the Answer remains the same. From the *human* throat of Jesus came those final words of confidence: "Father, into thy hands I commend my spirit." In His humanity, Jesus was near death, but His confidence held because He *knew* the Father.

Ours can hold, too, *if* we know Him.

If you do not know Him, *turn*. Even without a word, turn. You will find Him there—the Son of God—offering you not only forgiveness, but friendship. ". . . I call you not servants . . . I have called you friends."

I call you to be My friend, He is saying. To enter into a shared silence of both suffering and joy—with Me.

It could be that the shared silence is His way of teaching us the language of Eternity.

In the face of this freeing potential, I *want* no pat answers.

Acknowledgements

I wish to thank Celestine Sibley for partial use of her column which appeared in the *Atlanta Constitution* and Eleanor Ratelle for the use of her material, some of which appeared in the *Miami Herald*. To each person, especially Frances Pitts, who permitted the sharing of their experiences, I am grateful. My mother and her neighbours, Nancy and Mary Jane Goshorn, gave me careful criticism, love, and encouragement, as did my fellow-writer, Joyce Blackburn.

A recent visit with my long-time friend, Ellen Riley Urquhart, through whom Christ found me, has further convinced me that God's joy can fill even a grieving human heart. Her late husband and my dear friend, Charles, is with the Lord now—and I see Christ's love in Ellen as never before.

Those who handle the difficult mechanics of typing an author's marked-up manuscript deserve high praise and gratitude. I give this with love to my wonderful assistant, Lorrie Carlson. Judy Markham's superb editing has made me "look good", and working with her on *No Pat Answers*, as with *The Unique World of Women*, has been a stimulating experience.